50 Ultra Cake Recipes for Home

By: Kelly Johnson

Table of Contents

- Classic Chocolate Cake
- Vanilla Bean Layer Cake
- Red Velvet Cake
- Lemon Drizzle Cake
- Carrot Cake with Cream Cheese Frosting
- Mocha Coffee Cake
- Strawberry Shortcake
- Peanut Butter Cup Cake
- German Chocolate Cake
- Coconut Cream Cake
- Marble Cake
- Pumpkin Spice Cake
- Banana Nut Cake
- Blueberry Lemon Cake
- Raspberry Almond Cake
- S'mores Cake
- Pistachio Cake
- Funfetti Cake
- Tiramisu Cake
- Salted Caramel Cake
- Mint Chocolate Cake
- Apple Cinnamon Cake
- Chocolate Hazelnut Cake
- Key Lime Cake
- Almond Cake with Raspberry Filling
- Gingerbread Cake
- Maple Pecan Cake
- Orange Blossom Cake
- Matcha Green Tea Cake
- White Chocolate and Raspberry Cake
- Toffee Cake
- Fig and Walnut Cake
- Cherry Almond Cake
- Hazelnut Mocha Cake
- Pear and Ginger Cake
- Chocolate Mint Cake

- Mocha Almond Cake
- Lemon Blueberry Bundt Cake
- Creamy Lime Cake
- Cinnamon Roll Cake
- Espresso Cake
- Chocolate Cherry Cake
- Pineapple Upside-Down Cake
- Champagne Cake
- Sweet Potato Cake
- Nutella Swirl Cake
- Strawberry Basil Cake
- Raspberry Lemonade Cake
- Cardamom Cake
- Dulce de Leche Cake

Classic Chocolate Cake

Ingredients:

For the Cake:

- 1 ¾ cups (220g) all-purpose flour
- 1 ½ cups (300g) granulated sugar
- ¾ cup (65g) unsweetened cocoa powder
- 1 ½ tsp baking powder
- 1 ½ tsp baking soda
- 1 tsp salt
- 2 large eggs
- 1 cup (240ml) whole milk
- ½ cup (120ml) vegetable oil
- 2 tsp vanilla extract
- 1 cup (240ml) boiling water

For the Frosting:

- ½ cup (115g) unsalted butter, softened
- 1 ¾ cups (220g) confectioners' sugar
- ¾ cup (65g) unsweetened cocoa powder
- ¼ cup (60ml) whole milk
- 2 tsp vanilla extract

Instructions:

1. Preheat the Oven:

- Preheat your oven to 350°F (175°C). Grease and flour two 9-inch round cake pans or line them with parchment paper.

2. Mix Dry Ingredients:

- In a large mixing bowl, sift together the flour, sugar, cocoa powder, baking powder, baking soda, and salt.

3. Combine Wet Ingredients:

- Add the eggs, milk, oil, and vanilla extract to the dry ingredients. Beat on medium speed until well combined.

4. Add Boiling Water:

- Gradually stir in the boiling water until the batter is smooth. It will be quite thin, but that's okay.

5. Bake the Cake:

- Divide the batter evenly between the prepared pans. Bake for 30-35 minutes, or until a toothpick inserted into the center comes out clean.

6. Cool the Cake:

- Allow the cakes to cool in the pans for 10 minutes, then turn them out onto a wire rack to cool completely.

7. Prepare the Frosting:

- In a medium bowl, beat the butter until creamy. Gradually add the confectioners' sugar and cocoa powder, mixing on low speed until well blended. Add the milk and vanilla extract, and beat on high speed until the frosting is light and fluffy.

8. Frost the Cake:

- Once the cakes are completely cool, spread a layer of frosting on top of one cake layer, then place the second layer on top. Frost the top and sides of the cake with the remaining frosting.

9. Serve and Enjoy:

- Slice and serve. Enjoy your classic chocolate cake!

Feel free to add any decorations or toppings you like, such as chocolate shavings or sprinkles!

Vanilla Bean Layer Cake

Ingredients:

For the Cake:

- 2 ½ cups (310g) all-purpose flour
- 2 ½ tsp baking powder
- ½ tsp salt
- 1 cup (230g) unsalted butter, softened
- 1 ¾ cups (350g) granulated sugar
- 4 large eggs
- 1 cup (240ml) whole milk
- ½ cup (120ml) sour cream
- 2 tsp vanilla bean paste (or 1 tbsp vanilla extract)

For the Frosting:

- 1 cup (230g) unsalted butter, softened
- 4 cups (500g) confectioners' sugar
- ¼ cup (60ml) whole milk
- 2 tsp vanilla bean paste (or 1 tbsp vanilla extract)

Instructions:

1. Preheat the Oven:

- Preheat your oven to 350°F (175°C). Grease and flour three 8-inch round cake pans or line them with parchment paper.

2. Prepare the Cake Batter:

- In a medium bowl, sift together the flour, baking powder, and salt. Set aside.
- In a large mixing bowl, cream the butter and sugar together until light and fluffy, about 3-4 minutes.
- Add the eggs one at a time, beating well after each addition.
- Mix in the vanilla bean paste (or vanilla extract).
- Alternately add the flour mixture and the milk, starting and ending with the flour mixture. Beat just until combined.
- Fold in the sour cream until the batter is smooth.

3. Bake the Cake:

- Divide the batter evenly among the prepared pans.
- Bake for 25-30 minutes, or until a toothpick inserted into the center comes out clean.

- Allow the cakes to cool in the pans for 10 minutes, then turn them out onto a wire rack to cool completely.

4. Prepare the Frosting:

- In a medium bowl, beat the butter until creamy.
- Gradually add the confectioners' sugar, mixing on low speed until well blended.
- Add the milk and vanilla bean paste (or vanilla extract), and beat on high speed until the frosting is light and fluffy.

5. Assemble the Cake:

- Once the cakes are completely cool, place one cake layer on a serving plate or cake stand.
- Spread a layer of frosting on top of the first layer.
- Place the second cake layer on top and frost the top and sides of the cake.
- Repeat with the third layer and frost the entire cake smoothly.

6. Decorate and Serve:

- Decorate as desired. You can add sprinkles, fresh fruit, or other toppings if you like.
- Slice and serve. Enjoy your vanilla bean layer cake!

This cake is wonderfully light and flavorful, thanks to the vanilla bean paste. Perfect for birthdays, celebrations, or just a treat!

Red Velvet Cake

Ingredients:

For the Cake:

- 2 ½ cups (310g) all-purpose flour
- 1 ½ cups (300g) granulated sugar
- 1 tsp baking powder
- 1 tsp baking soda
- ½ tsp salt
- 1 cup (240ml) vegetable oil
- 1 cup (240ml) buttermilk, room temperature
- 2 large eggs
- 2 tbsp (15g) cocoa powder
- 2 tbsp (30ml) red food coloring (liquid or gel)
- 1 tsp vanilla extract
- 1 tsp white vinegar

For the Cream Cheese Frosting:

- 1 cup (230g) unsalted butter, softened
- 8 oz (225g) cream cheese, softened
- 4 cups (500g) confectioners' sugar
- 1 tsp vanilla extract

Instructions:

1. Preheat the Oven:

- Preheat your oven to 350°F (175°C). Grease and flour two 9-inch round cake pans or line them with parchment paper.

2. Prepare the Cake Batter:

- In a medium bowl, sift together the flour, sugar, baking powder, baking soda, and salt.
- In a large mixing bowl, combine the oil, buttermilk, eggs, cocoa powder, red food coloring, vanilla extract, and vinegar. Mix well.
- Gradually add the dry ingredients to the wet ingredients, mixing on low speed until just combined. Do not overmix.

3. Bake the Cake:

- Divide the batter evenly between the prepared pans.
- Bake for 25-30 minutes, or until a toothpick inserted into the center comes out clean.

- Allow the cakes to cool in the pans for 10 minutes, then turn them out onto a wire rack to cool completely.

4. Prepare the Cream Cheese Frosting:

- In a large mixing bowl, beat the softened butter and cream cheese until smooth and creamy.
- Gradually add the confectioners' sugar, mixing on low speed until fully incorporated.
- Add the vanilla extract and beat on high speed until the frosting is light and fluffy.

5. Assemble the Cake:

- Once the cakes are completely cool, place one cake layer on a serving plate or cake stand.
- Spread a layer of cream cheese frosting on top of the first layer.
- Place the second cake layer on top and frost the top and sides of the cake with the remaining cream cheese frosting.

6. Decorate and Serve:

- Decorate with any additional toppings or decorations you like, such as red velvet crumbs, edible glitter, or fresh berries.
- Slice and serve. Enjoy your red velvet cake!

This cake is known for its striking color and deliciously tangy cream cheese frosting. Perfect for special occasions or a delightful treat!

Lemon Drizzle Cake

Ingredients:

For the Cake:

- 1 ½ cups (190g) all-purpose flour
- 1 ½ tsp baking powder
- ¼ tsp salt
- ½ cup (115g) unsalted butter, softened
- 1 cup (200g) granulated sugar
- 2 large eggs
- ½ cup (120ml) whole milk
- ¼ cup (60ml) fresh lemon juice
- Zest of 2 lemons
- 1 tsp vanilla extract

For the Lemon Drizzle:

- ¼ cup (60ml) fresh lemon juice
- ½ cup (100g) granulated sugar

For the Glaze (optional):

- 1 cup (120g) confectioners' sugar
- 2-3 tbsp fresh lemon juice

Instructions:

1. Preheat the Oven:

- Preheat your oven to 350°F (175°C). Grease and flour a loaf pan (8.5x4.5 inches) or line it with parchment paper.

2. Prepare the Cake Batter:

- In a medium bowl, whisk together the flour, baking powder, and salt.
- In a large mixing bowl, cream the softened butter and granulated sugar together until light and fluffy, about 3-4 minutes.
- Add the eggs one at a time, beating well after each addition.
- Mix in the lemon zest and vanilla extract.
- Alternately add the dry ingredients and the milk to the butter mixture, starting and ending with the dry ingredients. Mix until just combined.
- Stir in the lemon juice until the batter is smooth.

3. Bake the Cake:

- Pour the batter into the prepared loaf pan.
- Bake for 50-60 minutes, or until a toothpick inserted into the center comes out clean.
- Allow the cake to cool in the pan for 10 minutes, then transfer to a wire rack to cool completely.

4. Prepare the Lemon Drizzle:

- While the cake is cooling, prepare the lemon drizzle. In a small saucepan, combine the lemon juice and granulated sugar.
- Cook over medium heat, stirring constantly, until the sugar has dissolved and the mixture is slightly thickened.
- Remove from heat and let it cool slightly.

5. Apply the Drizzle:

- Once the cake is completely cool, place it on a serving plate.
- Use a skewer or toothpick to poke holes all over the top of the cake.
- Pour the lemon drizzle evenly over the top of the cake, allowing it to soak into the holes.

6. Prepare the Glaze (Optional):

- If you'd like a sweeter, thicker glaze, mix the confectioners' sugar with 2-3 tablespoons of lemon juice until smooth. Drizzle over the cake once the lemon drizzle has set.

7. Serve:

- Slice and enjoy your lemon drizzle cake. It's perfect with a cup of tea or coffee!

This cake is delightfully tangy and sweet, with a moist crumb and a burst of lemon flavor. Enjoy!

Carrot Cake with Cream Cheese Frosting

Ingredients:

For the Carrot Cake:

- 2 cups (250g) all-purpose flour
- 2 tsp baking powder
- 1 ½ tsp baking soda
- ½ tsp salt
- 1 tsp ground cinnamon
- ½ tsp ground nutmeg
- ¼ tsp ground cloves
- 1 cup (200g) granulated sugar
- ½ cup (100g) packed light brown sugar
- 1 cup (240ml) vegetable oil
- 4 large eggs
- 2 cups (240g) grated carrots (about 3 medium carrots)
- ½ cup (80g) crushed pineapple, drained
- ½ cup (80g) chopped walnuts or pecans (optional)
- ½ cup (75g) raisins (optional)
- 1 tsp vanilla extract

For the Cream Cheese Frosting:

- 8 oz (225g) cream cheese, softened
- ½ cup (115g) unsalted butter, softened
- 4 cups (500g) confectioners' sugar
- 1 tsp vanilla extract

Instructions:

1. Preheat the Oven:

- Preheat your oven to 350°F (175°C). Grease and flour two 9-inch round cake pans or line them with parchment paper.

2. Prepare the Carrot Cake Batter:

- In a medium bowl, whisk together the flour, baking powder, baking soda, salt, cinnamon, nutmeg, and cloves.
- In a large mixing bowl, beat the granulated sugar, brown sugar, and oil together until well combined.
- Add the eggs one at a time, beating well after each addition.
- Mix in the vanilla extract.

- Gradually add the dry ingredients to the wet ingredients, mixing on low speed until just combined.
- Stir in the grated carrots, crushed pineapple, walnuts or pecans (if using), and raisins (if using) until evenly distributed.

3. Bake the Cake:

- Divide the batter evenly between the prepared pans.
- Bake for 25-30 minutes, or until a toothpick inserted into the center of the cakes comes out clean.
- Allow the cakes to cool in the pans for 10 minutes, then turn them out onto a wire rack to cool completely.

4. Prepare the Cream Cheese Frosting:

- In a large mixing bowl, beat the cream cheese and butter together until smooth and creamy.
- Gradually add the confectioners' sugar, mixing on low speed until fully incorporated.
- Add the vanilla extract and beat on high speed until the frosting is light and fluffy.

5. Assemble the Cake:

- Once the cakes are completely cool, place one cake layer on a serving plate or cake stand.
- Spread a layer of cream cheese frosting on top of the first layer.
- Place the second cake layer on top and frost the top and sides of the cake with the remaining cream cheese frosting.

6. Decorate and Serve:

- Decorate with additional chopped nuts, shredded coconut, or carrot decorations if desired.
- Slice and serve. Enjoy your moist and flavorful carrot cake with creamy frosting!

This carrot cake is wonderfully spiced, moist, and complemented perfectly by the rich cream cheese frosting. It's a classic favorite that's sure to please any crowd!

Mocha Coffee Cake

Ingredients:

For the Cake:

- 1 ¾ cups (220g) all-purpose flour
- 1 cup (200g) granulated sugar
- ½ cup (100g) packed light brown sugar
- ½ cup (45g) unsweetened cocoa powder
- 1 tsp baking powder
- 1 tsp baking soda
- ¼ tsp salt
- ½ cup (120ml) hot brewed coffee (strong)
- ½ cup (120ml) buttermilk (or whole milk)
- ½ cup (115g) unsalted butter, softened
- 2 large eggs
- 1 tsp vanilla extract

For the Streusel Topping:

- ¼ cup (50g) granulated sugar
- ¼ cup (50g) packed light brown sugar
- ¼ cup (30g) all-purpose flour
- 2 tbsp (15g) unsweetened cocoa powder
- ¼ cup (60g) unsalted butter, cold and cut into small pieces

For the Coffee Glaze (Optional):

- ½ cup (60g) confectioners' sugar
- 1-2 tbsp brewed coffee (adjust to desired consistency)

Instructions:

1. Preheat the Oven:

- Preheat your oven to 350°F (175°C). Grease and flour a 9-inch round cake pan or line it with parchment paper.

2. Prepare the Cake Batter:

- In a medium bowl, sift together the flour, granulated sugar, brown sugar, cocoa powder, baking powder, baking soda, and salt.
- In a separate bowl, mix the hot brewed coffee, buttermilk, and vanilla extract.
- In a large mixing bowl, cream the softened butter until light and fluffy.
- Add the eggs one at a time, beating well after each addition.

- Gradually add the dry ingredients to the butter mixture, alternating with the coffee mixture. Begin and end with the dry ingredients. Mix until just combined.

3. Prepare the Streusel Topping:

- In a medium bowl, combine the granulated sugar, brown sugar, flour, and cocoa powder.
- Cut in the cold butter using a pastry cutter or your fingers until the mixture resembles coarse crumbs.

4. Assemble the Cake:

- Pour half of the cake batter into the prepared pan and spread it evenly.
- Sprinkle half of the streusel topping over the batter.
- Pour the remaining batter on top and spread evenly.
- Sprinkle the remaining streusel topping over the top layer of batter.

5. Bake the Cake:

- Bake for 35-40 minutes, or until a toothpick inserted into the center comes out clean.
- Allow the cake to cool in the pan for 10 minutes, then transfer to a wire rack to cool completely.

6. Prepare the Coffee Glaze (Optional):

- In a small bowl, whisk together the confectioners' sugar and brewed coffee until smooth. Adjust the amount of coffee to reach your desired glaze consistency.

7. Drizzle the Glaze:

- Once the cake is completely cool, drizzle the coffee glaze over the top if desired.

8. Serve:

- Slice and enjoy your Mocha Coffee Cake with a cup of coffee or tea.

This Mocha Coffee Cake is perfect for coffee lovers, with its rich chocolate flavor and hint of coffee, topped with a sweet streusel. Enjoy!

Strawberry Shortcake

Ingredients:

For the Shortcake:

- 2 cups (250g) all-purpose flour
- ¼ cup (50g) granulated sugar
- 1 tbsp baking powder
- ½ tsp salt
- ½ cup (115g) unsalted butter, cold and cut into small pieces
- 2/3 cup (160ml) whole milk
- 1 large egg
- 1 tsp vanilla extract

For the Strawberries:

- 4 cups (600g) fresh strawberries, hulled and sliced
- ¼ cup (50g) granulated sugar

For the Whipped Cream:

- 1 cup (240ml) heavy cream
- 2 tbsp granulated sugar
- 1 tsp vanilla extract

Instructions:

1. Prepare the Strawberries:

- In a large bowl, combine the sliced strawberries and granulated sugar. Toss to coat.
- Let the strawberries sit for at least 30 minutes to macerate, which will release their juices and create a syrupy mixture.

2. Preheat the Oven:

- Preheat your oven to 425°F (220°C). Grease and flour an 8-inch round cake pan or line it with parchment paper.

3. Make the Shortcake:

- In a large bowl, whisk together the flour, sugar, baking powder, and salt.
- Cut in the cold butter using a pastry cutter or your fingers until the mixture resembles coarse crumbs.
- In a separate bowl, whisk together the milk, egg, and vanilla extract.
- Pour the milk mixture into the flour mixture and stir until just combined. Do not overmix.

4. Bake the Shortcake:

- Transfer the dough to a lightly floured surface and gently knead a few times. Pat it into a 1-inch thick round shape.
- Cut into 8 wedges (or use a biscuit cutter to make round shortcakes) and place on the prepared baking pan.
- Bake for 12-15 minutes, or until the shortcakes are golden brown.
- Allow the shortcakes to cool slightly on a wire rack.

5. Prepare the Whipped Cream:

- In a large mixing bowl, beat the heavy cream, granulated sugar, and vanilla extract with an electric mixer until stiff peaks form.

6. Assemble the Strawberry Shortcake:

- Slice the shortcakes in half horizontally.
- Spoon some of the macerated strawberries onto the bottom half of each shortcake.
- Top with a dollop of whipped cream.
- Place the top half of the shortcake over the whipped cream.
- Add more strawberries and whipped cream on top if desired.

7. Serve:

- Serve immediately and enjoy your delicious homemade Strawberry Shortcake!

This Strawberry Shortcake recipe is simple yet classic, perfect for showcasing fresh strawberries in a delightful dessert. Enjoy!

Peanut Butter Cup Cake

Ingredients:

For the Cake:

- 1 ¾ cups (220g) all-purpose flour
- 1 ½ tsp baking powder
- 1 ½ tsp baking soda
- ¼ tsp salt
- ½ cup (115g) unsalted butter, softened
- 1 cup (200g) granulated sugar
- ½ cup (100g) packed light brown sugar
- 2 large eggs
- ½ cup (120ml) creamy peanut butter
- 1 cup (240ml) whole milk
- 1 tsp vanilla extract
- ½ cup (120ml) hot water

For the Peanut Butter Frosting:

- 1 cup (230g) unsalted butter, softened
- 1 cup (250g) creamy peanut butter
- 3-4 cups (375-500g) confectioners' sugar (to taste)
- ¼ cup (60ml) whole milk
- 1 tsp vanilla extract

For the Chocolate Ganache:

- ½ cup (120ml) heavy cream
- 1 cup (170g) semisweet chocolate chips

For Decoration (Optional):

- Mini peanut butter cups, chopped
- Chocolate shavings or sprinkles

Instructions:

1. Preheat the Oven:

- Preheat your oven to 350°F (175°C). Grease and flour two 9-inch round cake pans or line them with parchment paper.

2. Prepare the Cake Batter:

- In a medium bowl, whisk together the flour, baking powder, baking soda, and salt.

- In a large mixing bowl, cream the softened butter, granulated sugar, and brown sugar together until light and fluffy.
- Add the eggs one at a time, beating well after each addition.
- Mix in the peanut butter and vanilla extract.
- Gradually add the dry ingredients to the butter mixture, alternating with the milk. Begin and end with the dry ingredients. Mix until just combined.
- Stir in the hot water until the batter is smooth (it will be thin, but that's okay).

3. Bake the Cake:

- Divide the batter evenly between the prepared pans.
- Bake for 30-35 minutes, or until a toothpick inserted into the center comes out clean.
- Allow the cakes to cool in the pans for 10 minutes, then turn them out onto a wire rack to cool completely.

4. Prepare the Peanut Butter Frosting:

- In a large mixing bowl, beat the softened butter and peanut butter until smooth and creamy.
- Gradually add the confectioners' sugar, mixing on low speed until incorporated.
- Add the milk and vanilla extract, and beat on high speed until the frosting is light and fluffy.

5. Prepare the Chocolate Ganache:

- In a small saucepan, heat the heavy cream over medium heat until just beginning to simmer.
- Remove from heat and add the chocolate chips. Let sit for 2 minutes, then stir until smooth.
- Let the ganache cool slightly before using.

6. Assemble the Cake:

- Place one cake layer on a serving plate or cake stand.
- Spread a layer of peanut butter frosting on top.
- Place the second cake layer on top and frost the top and sides of the cake with the remaining peanut butter frosting.
- Pour the chocolate ganache over the top of the cake, letting it drizzle down the sides.

7. Decorate:

- Garnish with chopped mini peanut butter cups and chocolate shavings or sprinkles if desired.

8. Serve:

- Slice and enjoy your indulgent Peanut Butter Cup Cake!

This cake is a chocolate-peanut butter lover's dream, featuring rich flavors and a decadent combination of frosting and ganache. Enjoy!

German Chocolate Cake

Ingredients:

For the Cake:

- 1 ¾ cups (220g) all-purpose flour
- 1 cup (200g) granulated sugar
- ½ cup (100g) packed light brown sugar
- ¾ cup (65g) unsweetened cocoa powder
- 1 ½ tsp baking powder
- 1 ½ tsp baking soda
- ½ tsp salt
- ½ cup (120ml) boiling water
- ½ cup (120ml) buttermilk (or whole milk)
- ½ cup (115g) unsalted butter, softened
- 2 large eggs
- 1 tsp vanilla extract
- 1 cup (240ml) hot brewed coffee (or use hot water if preferred)

For the Coconut-Pecan Frosting:

- 1 cup (240ml) evaporated milk
- 1 cup (200g) granulated sugar
- 3 large egg yolks
- ½ cup (115g) unsalted butter
- 1 tsp vanilla extract
- 1 ½ cups (150g) sweetened shredded coconut
- 1 cup (120g) chopped pecans

Instructions:

1. Preheat the Oven:

- Preheat your oven to 350°F (175°C). Grease and flour three 9-inch round cake pans or line them with parchment paper.

2. Prepare the Cake Batter:

- In a large mixing bowl, sift together the flour, granulated sugar, brown sugar, cocoa powder, baking powder, baking soda, and salt.
- In a separate bowl, mix the boiling water with the cocoa powder until smooth. Let it cool slightly.
- In another bowl, whisk together the buttermilk, softened butter, eggs, and vanilla extract.
- Gradually add the dry ingredients to the wet ingredients, mixing until just combined.
- Stir in the hot coffee (or water) and cocoa mixture until smooth.

- Divide the batter evenly between the prepared pans.

3. Bake the Cake:

- Bake for 25-30 minutes, or until a toothpick inserted into the center of the cakes comes out clean.
- Allow the cakes to cool in the pans for 10 minutes, then turn them out onto a wire rack to cool completely.

4. Prepare the Coconut-Pecan Frosting:

- In a medium saucepan, combine the evaporated milk, granulated sugar, and egg yolks. Cook over medium heat, whisking constantly, until the mixture begins to thicken and reaches a custard-like consistency (about 10-12 minutes).
- Remove from heat and stir in the butter, vanilla extract, shredded coconut, and chopped pecans.
- Let the frosting cool and set before using (it will thicken further as it cools).

5. Assemble the Cake:

- Once the cakes are completely cool, place one cake layer on a serving plate or cake stand.
- Spread a layer of coconut-pecan frosting on top.
- Place the second cake layer on top and frost the top and sides of the cake with the remaining frosting.
- If desired, you can garnish the cake with additional coconut and pecans.

6. Serve:

- Slice and enjoy your rich and decadent German Chocolate Cake!

This cake is famous for its distinctive coconut-pecan frosting and moist chocolate cake layers, making it a delicious treat for any special occasion. Enjoy!

Coconut Cream Cake

Ingredients:

For the Cake:

- 1 ½ cups (190g) all-purpose flour
- 1 ½ tsp baking powder
- ½ tsp baking soda
- ¼ tsp salt
- ½ cup (115g) unsalted butter, softened
- 1 cup (200g) granulated sugar
- 2 large eggs
- 1 cup (240ml) sour cream
- 1/3 cup (80ml) coconut milk (canned or carton)
- 1 tsp vanilla extract
- 1 cup (100g) sweetened shredded coconut (toasted or untoasted, as preferred)

For the Coconut Cream Frosting:

- 1 cup (240ml) heavy cream
- ½ cup (50g) confectioners' sugar
- 1 tsp vanilla extract
- 1 cup (100g) sweetened shredded coconut (toasted for added flavor, if desired)

For Decoration (Optional):

- Additional sweetened shredded coconut, toasted or untoasted
- Fresh coconut flakes or coconut chips

Instructions:

1. Preheat the Oven:

- Preheat your oven to 350°F (175°C). Grease and flour two 9-inch round cake pans or line them with parchment paper.

2. Prepare the Cake Batter:

- In a medium bowl, whisk together the flour, baking powder, baking soda, and salt.
- In a large mixing bowl, cream the softened butter and granulated sugar together until light and fluffy.
- Add the eggs one at a time, beating well after each addition.
- Mix in the vanilla extract.
- Gradually add the dry ingredients to the butter mixture, alternating with the sour cream and coconut milk. Begin and end with the dry ingredients. Mix until just combined.

- Stir in the shredded coconut until evenly distributed.

3. Bake the Cake:

- Divide the batter evenly between the prepared pans.
- Bake for 25-30 minutes, or until a toothpick inserted into the center of the cakes comes out clean.
- Allow the cakes to cool in the pans for 10 minutes, then turn them out onto a wire rack to cool completely.

4. Prepare the Coconut Cream Frosting:

- In a large mixing bowl, beat the heavy cream, confectioners' sugar, and vanilla extract until stiff peaks form.
- Fold in the shredded coconut until evenly distributed.

5. Assemble the Cake:

- Once the cakes are completely cool, place one cake layer on a serving plate or cake stand.
- Spread a layer of coconut cream frosting on top of the first layer.
- Place the second cake layer on top and frost the top and sides of the cake with the remaining coconut cream frosting.

6. Decorate (Optional):

- Garnish the cake with additional shredded coconut, toasted or untoasted, and fresh coconut flakes or coconut chips if desired.

7. Serve:

- Slice and enjoy your Coconut Cream Cake!

This Coconut Cream Cake is light, moist, and packed with coconut flavor, perfect for a tropical treat or any special occasion. Enjoy!

Marble Cake

Ingredients:

For the Cake:

- 1 ¾ cups (220g) all-purpose flour
- 1 ½ tsp baking powder
- ¼ tsp salt
- ½ cup (115g) unsalted butter, softened
- 1 cup (200g) granulated sugar
- 2 large eggs
- 1 tsp vanilla extract
- ½ cup (120ml) milk
- ¼ cup (60ml) sour cream or plain yogurt

For the Chocolate Batter:

- ¼ cup (20g) unsweetened cocoa powder
- ¼ cup (60ml) boiling water

Instructions:

1. Preheat the Oven:

- Preheat your oven to 350°F (175°C). Grease and flour a 9-inch round cake pan or line it with parchment paper.

2. Prepare the Cake Batter:

- In a medium bowl, whisk together the flour, baking powder, and salt.
- In a large mixing bowl, cream the softened butter and granulated sugar together until light and fluffy.
- Add the eggs one at a time, beating well after each addition.
- Mix in the vanilla extract.
- Gradually add the dry ingredients to the butter mixture, alternating with the milk and sour cream. Begin and end with the dry ingredients. Mix until just combined.

3. Prepare the Chocolate Batter:

- In a small bowl, mix the cocoa powder with boiling water until smooth and well combined.

4. Combine the Batters:

- Divide the vanilla batter evenly between two bowls.
- Add the chocolate mixture to one of the bowls and mix until combined.

5. Marble the Cake:

- Spoon alternating dollops of vanilla and chocolate batters into the prepared pan.
- Using a knife or a skewer, gently swirl the batters together to create a marbled effect. Be careful not to over-swirl; you want distinct streaks of chocolate and vanilla.

6. Bake the Cake:

- Bake for 30-35 minutes, or until a toothpick inserted into the center comes out clean.
- Allow the cake to cool in the pan for 10 minutes, then transfer to a wire rack to cool completely.

7. Serve:

- Once completely cool, slice and enjoy your beautifully marbled cake!

This Marble Cake is perfect for those who can't decide between chocolate and vanilla, offering the best of both flavors in a single, delicious dessert. Enjoy!

Pumpkin Spice Cake

Ingredients:

For the Cake:

- 1 ½ cups (190g) all-purpose flour
- 1 tsp baking powder
- 1 tsp baking soda
- ½ tsp salt
- 1 tsp ground cinnamon
- ½ tsp ground nutmeg
- ½ tsp ground ginger
- ¼ tsp ground cloves
- ½ cup (115g) unsalted butter, softened
- 1 cup (200g) granulated sugar
- ½ cup (100g) packed light brown sugar
- 2 large eggs
- 1 cup (240ml) canned pumpkin (not pumpkin pie filling)
- ½ cup (120ml) buttermilk (or whole milk)
- 1 tsp vanilla extract

For the Cream Cheese Frosting:

- 8 oz (225g) cream cheese, softened
- ½ cup (115g) unsalted butter, softened
- 4 cups (500g) confectioners' sugar
- 1 tsp vanilla extract
- Optional: 1-2 tbsp milk or cream (to adjust consistency)

For Decoration (Optional):

- Ground cinnamon
- Chopped pecans or walnuts

Instructions:

1. Preheat the Oven:

- Preheat your oven to 350°F (175°C). Grease and flour two 9-inch round cake pans or line them with parchment paper.

2. Prepare the Cake Batter:

- In a medium bowl, whisk together the flour, baking powder, baking soda, salt, cinnamon, nutmeg, ginger, and cloves.

- In a large mixing bowl, cream the softened butter, granulated sugar, and brown sugar together until light and fluffy.
- Add the eggs one at a time, beating well after each addition.
- Mix in the vanilla extract and pumpkin until well combined.
- Gradually add the dry ingredients to the butter mixture, alternating with the buttermilk. Begin and end with the dry ingredients. Mix until just combined.

3. Bake the Cake:

- Divide the batter evenly between the prepared pans.
- Bake for 25-30 minutes, or until a toothpick inserted into the center comes out clean.
- Allow the cakes to cool in the pans for 10 minutes, then turn them out onto a wire rack to cool completely.

4. Prepare the Cream Cheese Frosting:

- In a large mixing bowl, beat the cream cheese and butter together until smooth and creamy.
- Gradually add the confectioners' sugar, mixing on low speed until fully incorporated.
- Mix in the vanilla extract. If the frosting is too thick, add 1-2 tablespoons of milk or cream to reach your desired consistency.

5. Assemble the Cake:

- Once the cakes are completely cool, place one cake layer on a serving plate or cake stand.
- Spread a layer of cream cheese frosting on top of the first layer.
- Place the second cake layer on top and frost the top and sides of the cake with the remaining cream cheese frosting.

6. Decorate (Optional):

- Sprinkle the top with ground cinnamon or garnish with chopped pecans or walnuts if desired.

7. Serve:

- Slice and enjoy your flavorful Pumpkin Spice Cake!

This Pumpkin Spice Cake is moist, flavorful, and topped with creamy frosting, making it a perfect treat for fall gatherings or any time of year. Enjoy!

Banana Nut Cake

Ingredients:

For the Cake:

- 1 ½ cups (190g) all-purpose flour
- 1 tsp baking powder
- ½ tsp baking soda
- ¼ tsp salt
- ½ tsp ground cinnamon (optional)
- ½ cup (115g) unsalted butter, softened
- 1 cup (200g) granulated sugar
- 2 large eggs
- 1 cup (240ml) mashed ripe bananas (about 2-3 medium bananas)
- ½ cup (120ml) buttermilk (or whole milk)
- 1 tsp vanilla extract
- ½ cup (60g) chopped walnuts or pecans

For the Cream Cheese Frosting:

- 8 oz (225g) cream cheese, softened
- ½ cup (115g) unsalted butter, softened
- 4 cups (500g) confectioners' sugar
- 1 tsp vanilla extract

For Decoration (Optional):

- Additional chopped walnuts or pecans
- Sliced banana for garnish

Instructions:

1. Preheat the Oven:

- Preheat your oven to 350°F (175°C). Grease and flour two 9-inch round cake pans or line them with parchment paper.

2. Prepare the Cake Batter:

- In a medium bowl, whisk together the flour, baking powder, baking soda, salt, and cinnamon (if using).
- In a large mixing bowl, cream the softened butter and granulated sugar together until light and fluffy.
- Add the eggs one at a time, beating well after each addition.
- Mix in the mashed bananas and vanilla extract.

- Gradually add the dry ingredients to the butter mixture, alternating with the buttermilk. Begin and end with the dry ingredients. Mix until just combined.
- Fold in the chopped nuts until evenly distributed.

3. Bake the Cake:

- Divide the batter evenly between the prepared pans.
- Bake for 25-30 minutes, or until a toothpick inserted into the center comes out clean.
- Allow the cakes to cool in the pans for 10 minutes, then turn them out onto a wire rack to cool completely.

4. Prepare the Cream Cheese Frosting:

- In a large mixing bowl, beat the cream cheese and butter together until smooth and creamy.
- Gradually add the confectioners' sugar, mixing on low speed until fully incorporated.
- Mix in the vanilla extract.

5. Assemble the Cake:

- Once the cakes are completely cool, place one cake layer on a serving plate or cake stand.
- Spread a layer of cream cheese frosting on top of the first layer.
- Place the second cake layer on top and frost the top and sides of the cake with the remaining cream cheese frosting.

6. Decorate (Optional):

- Garnish with additional chopped walnuts or pecans and sliced banana if desired.

7. Serve:

- Slice and enjoy your moist and flavorful Banana Nut Cake!

This cake is perfect for banana lovers, offering a delightful combination of moist banana flavor and crunchy nuts, topped with creamy frosting. Enjoy!

Blueberry Lemon Cake

Ingredients:

For the Cake:

- 1 ½ cups (190g) all-purpose flour
- 1 ½ tsp baking powder
- ½ tsp baking soda
- ¼ tsp salt
- ½ cup (115g) unsalted butter, softened
- 1 cup (200g) granulated sugar
- 2 large eggs
- ½ cup (120ml) sour cream (or Greek yogurt)
- ¼ cup (60ml) whole milk
- 1 tbsp lemon zest (about 1 lemon)
- 2 tbsp lemon juice (about 1 lemon)
- 1 tsp vanilla extract
- 1 cup (150g) fresh blueberries (or frozen, do not thaw)

For the Lemon Glaze:

- 1 cup (125g) confectioners' sugar
- 2-3 tbsp lemon juice (adjust to desired consistency)
- Optional: Lemon zest for garnish

For Decoration (Optional):

- Fresh blueberries
- Lemon slices or lemon zest

Instructions:

1. Preheat the Oven:

- Preheat your oven to 350°F (175°C). Grease and flour an 8-inch round cake pan or line it with parchment paper.

2. Prepare the Cake Batter:

- In a medium bowl, whisk together the flour, baking powder, baking soda, and salt.
- In a large mixing bowl, cream the softened butter and granulated sugar together until light and fluffy.
- Add the eggs one at a time, beating well after each addition.
- Mix in the lemon zest, lemon juice, and vanilla extract.

- Gradually add the dry ingredients to the butter mixture, alternating with the sour cream and milk. Begin and end with the dry ingredients. Mix until just combined.
- Gently fold in the blueberries until evenly distributed (be careful not to overmix as it may break the berries).

3. Bake the Cake:

- Pour the batter into the prepared pan and smooth the top.
- Bake for 30-35 minutes, or until a toothpick inserted into the center comes out clean.
- Allow the cake to cool in the pan for 10 minutes, then turn it out onto a wire rack to cool completely.

4. Prepare the Lemon Glaze:

- In a small bowl, whisk together the confectioners' sugar and lemon juice until smooth. Adjust the consistency by adding more lemon juice if needed (it should be pourable but not too runny).

5. Glaze the Cake:

- Once the cake is completely cool, drizzle the lemon glaze over the top, allowing it to drip down the sides.

6. Decorate (Optional):

- Garnish with additional fresh blueberries and lemon slices or zest if desired.

7. Serve:

- Slice and enjoy your delicious Blueberry Lemon Cake!

This Blueberry Lemon Cake is a perfect balance of sweet and tangy, with juicy blueberries and a refreshing lemon glaze. Enjoy!

Raspberry Almond Cake

Ingredients:

For the Cake:

- 1 ¼ cups (155g) all-purpose flour
- 1 tsp baking powder
- ½ tsp baking soda
- ¼ tsp salt
- ½ cup (115g) unsalted butter, softened
- ¾ cup (150g) granulated sugar
- 2 large eggs
- ½ cup (120ml) sour cream (or Greek yogurt)
- ¼ cup (60ml) milk
- 1 tsp vanilla extract
- ¼ cup (40g) finely ground almonds (almond meal or almond flour)
- 1 cup (125g) fresh raspberries (or frozen, do not thaw)

For the Almond Glaze:

- 1 cup (125g) confectioners' sugar
- 2-3 tbsp milk (adjust to desired consistency)
- ¼ tsp almond extract

For Decoration (Optional):

- Sliced almonds
- Fresh raspberries
- Powdered sugar

Instructions:

1. Preheat the Oven:

- Preheat your oven to 350°F (175°C). Grease and flour an 8-inch round cake pan or line it with parchment paper.

2. Prepare the Cake Batter:

- In a medium bowl, whisk together the flour, baking powder, baking soda, and salt.
- In a large mixing bowl, cream the softened butter and granulated sugar together until light and fluffy.
- Add the eggs one at a time, beating well after each addition.
- Mix in the vanilla extract.

- Gradually add the dry ingredients to the butter mixture, alternating with the sour cream and milk. Begin and end with the dry ingredients. Mix until just combined.
- Gently fold in the finely ground almonds and raspberries until evenly distributed (be careful not to overmix as it may break the raspberries).

3. Bake the Cake:

- Pour the batter into the prepared pan and smooth the top.
- Bake for 25-30 minutes, or until a toothpick inserted into the center comes out clean.
- Allow the cake to cool in the pan for 10 minutes, then turn it out onto a wire rack to cool completely.

4. Prepare the Almond Glaze:

- In a small bowl, whisk together the confectioners' sugar, milk, and almond extract until smooth. Adjust the consistency by adding more milk if needed (it should be pourable but not too runny).

5. Glaze the Cake:

- Once the cake is completely cool, drizzle the almond glaze over the top, allowing it to drip down the sides.

6. Decorate (Optional):

- Garnish with sliced almonds, fresh raspberries, and a dusting of powdered sugar if desired.

7. Serve:

- Slice and enjoy your delightful Raspberry Almond Cake!

This cake is perfect for those who enjoy the combination of sweet raspberries and nutty almonds, offering a deliciously light and flavorful treat. Enjoy!

S'mores Cake

Ingredients:

For the Graham Cracker Cake Layers:

- 1 ½ cups (190g) all-purpose flour
- 1 cup (200g) granulated sugar
- 1 tsp baking powder
- ½ tsp baking soda
- ¼ tsp salt
- ½ cup (115g) unsalted butter, softened
- 2 large eggs
- 1 cup (240ml) milk
- 1 tsp vanilla extract
- 1 cup (100g) graham cracker crumbs

For the Chocolate Cake Layers:

- 1 ¼ cups (155g) all-purpose flour
- 1 cup (200g) granulated sugar
- ½ cup (45g) unsweetened cocoa powder
- 1 ½ tsp baking powder
- 1 tsp baking soda
- ¼ tsp salt
- ½ cup (120ml) vegetable oil
- 2 large eggs
- 1 cup (240ml) buttermilk
- 1 tsp vanilla extract
- ½ cup (120ml) hot water

For the Marshmallow Frosting:

- 1 cup (225g) unsalted butter, softened
- 1 cup (120g) confectioners' sugar
- 1 cup (80g) marshmallow fluff (or marshmallow creme)
- 1 tsp vanilla extract

For the Chocolate Ganache:

- ½ cup (120ml) heavy cream
- 1 cup (170g) semisweet chocolate chips

For Decoration (Optional):

- Graham cracker crumbs

- Mini marshmallows
- Chocolate bar pieces

Instructions:

1. Preheat the Oven:

- Preheat your oven to 350°F (175°C). Grease and flour two 9-inch round cake pans or line them with parchment paper.

2. Prepare the Graham Cracker Cake Layers:

- In a medium bowl, whisk together the flour, sugar, baking powder, baking soda, and salt.
- In a large mixing bowl, beat the softened butter until creamy. Add the eggs one at a time, beating well after each addition.
- Mix in the vanilla extract.
- Gradually add the dry ingredients to the butter mixture, alternating with the milk. Begin and end with the dry ingredients. Mix until just combined.
- Fold in the graham cracker crumbs until evenly distributed.

3. Prepare the Chocolate Cake Layers:

- In a medium bowl, whisk together the flour, sugar, cocoa powder, baking powder, baking soda, and salt.
- In a large mixing bowl, combine the oil, eggs, buttermilk, and vanilla extract. Gradually add the dry ingredients, mixing until combined.
- Stir in the hot water until the batter is smooth (it will be thin).

4. Bake the Cake Layers:

- Divide the graham cracker batter evenly between the prepared pans and smooth the tops.
- Pour the chocolate batter evenly over the graham cracker batter.
- Bake for 30-35 minutes, or until a toothpick inserted into the center comes out clean.
- Allow the cakes to cool in the pans for 10 minutes, then turn them out onto a wire rack to cool completely.

5. Prepare the Marshmallow Frosting:

- In a large mixing bowl, beat the softened butter until creamy.
- Gradually add the confectioners' sugar, mixing on low speed until combined.
- Mix in the marshmallow fluff and vanilla extract until smooth and fluffy.

6. Prepare the Chocolate Ganache:

- In a small saucepan, heat the heavy cream over medium heat until it begins to simmer.

- Remove from heat and add the chocolate chips. Let sit for 2 minutes, then stir until smooth.
- Allow the ganache to cool slightly before using.

7. Assemble the Cake:

- Once the cakes are completely cool, place one cake layer on a serving plate or cake stand.
- Spread a layer of marshmallow frosting on top.
- Place the second cake layer on top and frost the top and sides of the cake with the remaining marshmallow frosting.

8. Add the Chocolate Ganache:

- Pour the chocolate ganache over the top of the cake, allowing it to drip down the sides.

9. Decorate (Optional):

- Garnish with graham cracker crumbs, mini marshmallows, and chocolate bar pieces.

10. Serve:

- Slice and enjoy your decadent S'mores Cake!

This cake brings together the beloved flavors of s'mores into a rich, layered dessert that's perfect for any occasion. Enjoy!

Pistachio Cake

Ingredients:

For the Cake:

- 1 ½ cups (190g) all-purpose flour
- 1 tsp baking powder
- ½ tsp baking soda
- ¼ tsp salt
- ½ cup (115g) unsalted butter, softened
- 1 cup (200g) granulated sugar
- 3 large eggs
- 1 cup (240ml) buttermilk (or whole milk)
- 1 tsp vanilla extract
- ½ cup (60g) finely ground pistachios (pistachio meal)
- ¼ cup (30g) chopped pistachios (optional, for added texture)

For the Pistachio Frosting:

- 8 oz (225g) cream cheese, softened
- ½ cup (115g) unsalted butter, softened
- 3-4 cups (375-500g) confectioners' sugar
- ½ cup (60g) finely ground pistachios
- 1 tsp vanilla extract

For Decoration (Optional):

- Chopped pistachios
- Fresh mint leaves

Instructions:

1. Preheat the Oven:

- Preheat your oven to 350°F (175°C). Grease and flour two 8-inch round cake pans or line them with parchment paper.

2. Prepare the Cake Batter:

- In a medium bowl, whisk together the flour, baking powder, baking soda, and salt.
- In a large mixing bowl, cream the softened butter and granulated sugar together until light and fluffy.
- Add the eggs one at a time, beating well after each addition.
- Mix in the vanilla extract.

- Gradually add the dry ingredients to the butter mixture, alternating with the buttermilk. Begin and end with the dry ingredients. Mix until just combined.
- Gently fold in the finely ground pistachios and chopped pistachios if using.

3. Bake the Cake:

- Divide the batter evenly between the prepared pans and smooth the tops.
- Bake for 25-30 minutes, or until a toothpick inserted into the center comes out clean.
- Allow the cakes to cool in the pans for 10 minutes, then turn them out onto a wire rack to cool completely.

4. Prepare the Pistachio Frosting:

- In a large mixing bowl, beat the cream cheese and butter together until smooth and creamy.
- Gradually add the confectioners' sugar, mixing on low speed until fully incorporated.
- Mix in the finely ground pistachios and vanilla extract until smooth.

5. Assemble the Cake:

- Once the cakes are completely cool, place one cake layer on a serving plate or cake stand.
- Spread a layer of pistachio frosting on top.
- Place the second cake layer on top and frost the top and sides of the cake with the remaining pistachio frosting.

6. Decorate (Optional):

- Garnish with additional chopped pistachios and fresh mint leaves if desired.

7. Serve:

- Slice and enjoy your rich and nutty Pistachio Cake!

This cake is perfect for pistachio lovers, offering a delightful nutty flavor and a creamy frosting that complements the moist cake layers. Enjoy!

Funfetti Cake

Ingredients:

For the Cake:

- 2 ¾ cups (345g) all-purpose flour
- 1 ½ tsp baking powder
- ½ tsp baking soda
- ½ tsp salt
- ½ cup (115g) unsalted butter, softened
- 1 cup (200g) granulated sugar
- ½ cup (100g) packed light brown sugar
- 3 large eggs
- 1 cup (240ml) buttermilk (or whole milk)
- 1 tsp vanilla extract
- ½ cup (75g) rainbow sprinkles

For the Vanilla Buttercream Frosting:

- 1 cup (225g) unsalted butter, softened
- 4 cups (500g) confectioners' sugar
- 2-3 tbsp heavy cream (or milk)
- 1 tsp vanilla extract
- ¼ cup (30g) rainbow sprinkles (for decorating)

For Decoration (Optional):

- Additional rainbow sprinkles

Instructions:

1. Preheat the Oven:

- Preheat your oven to 350°F (175°C). Grease and flour two 9-inch round cake pans or line them with parchment paper.

2. Prepare the Cake Batter:

- In a medium bowl, whisk together the flour, baking powder, baking soda, and salt.
- In a large mixing bowl, cream the softened butter, granulated sugar, and brown sugar together until light and fluffy.
- Add the eggs one at a time, beating well after each addition.
- Mix in the vanilla extract.
- Gradually add the dry ingredients to the butter mixture, alternating with the buttermilk. Begin and end with the dry ingredients. Mix until just combined.

- Gently fold in the rainbow sprinkles until evenly distributed.

3. Bake the Cake:

- Divide the batter evenly between the prepared pans and smooth the tops.
- Bake for 25-30 minutes, or until a toothpick inserted into the center comes out clean.
- Allow the cakes to cool in the pans for 10 minutes, then turn them out onto a wire rack to cool completely.

4. Prepare the Vanilla Buttercream Frosting:

- In a large mixing bowl, beat the softened butter until creamy.
- Gradually add the confectioners' sugar, mixing on low speed until fully incorporated.
- Mix in the vanilla extract.
- Add 2-3 tablespoons of heavy cream (or milk) one tablespoon at a time until the frosting reaches your desired consistency. It should be smooth and spreadable.

5. Assemble the Cake:

- Once the cakes are completely cool, place one cake layer on a serving plate or cake stand.
- Spread a layer of vanilla buttercream frosting on top.
- Place the second cake layer on top and frost the top and sides of the cake with the remaining vanilla buttercream frosting.

6. Decorate:

- Garnish with additional rainbow sprinkles for a festive touch.

7. Serve:

- Slice and enjoy your fun and colorful Funfetti Cake!

This Funfetti Cake is perfect for birthdays, celebrations, or anytime you want to add a bit of fun and cheer to your day. Enjoy!

Tiramisu Cake

Ingredients:

For the Cake:

- 1 ½ cups (190g) all-purpose flour
- 1 ½ tsp baking powder
- ½ tsp baking soda
- ¼ tsp salt
- ½ cup (115g) unsalted butter, softened
- 1 cup (200g) granulated sugar
- 2 large eggs
- 1 cup (240ml) sour cream (or Greek yogurt)
- 1 tsp vanilla extract
- ¼ cup (60ml) brewed espresso, cooled

For the Coffee Syrup:

- ½ cup (120ml) brewed espresso or strong coffee
- ¼ cup (50g) granulated sugar
- 2 tbsp coffee liqueur (optional, such as Kahlua)

For the Mascarpone Frosting:

- 8 oz (225g) mascarpone cheese, softened
- ½ cup (115g) unsalted butter, softened
- 1 cup (120g) confectioners' sugar
- 1 tsp vanilla extract
- 2 tbsp brewed espresso, cooled

For Decoration (Optional):

- Unsweetened cocoa powder
- Chocolate shavings or grated chocolate

Instructions:

1. Preheat the Oven:

- Preheat your oven to 350°F (175°C). Grease and flour two 9-inch round cake pans or line them with parchment paper.

2. Prepare the Cake Batter:

- In a medium bowl, whisk together the flour, baking powder, baking soda, and salt.

- In a large mixing bowl, cream the softened butter and granulated sugar together until light and fluffy.
- Add the eggs one at a time, beating well after each addition.
- Mix in the vanilla extract.
- Gradually add the dry ingredients to the butter mixture, alternating with the sour cream. Begin and end with the dry ingredients. Mix until just combined.
- Fold in the brewed espresso until evenly distributed.

3. Bake the Cake:

- Divide the batter evenly between the prepared pans and smooth the tops.
- Bake for 25-30 minutes, or until a toothpick inserted into the center comes out clean.
- Allow the cakes to cool in the pans for 10 minutes, then turn them out onto a wire rack to cool completely.

4. Prepare the Coffee Syrup:

- In a small saucepan, heat the brewed espresso and granulated sugar over medium heat, stirring until the sugar dissolves. Remove from heat and let cool. Stir in the coffee liqueur if using.

5. Prepare the Mascarpone Frosting:

- In a large mixing bowl, beat the mascarpone cheese and butter together until smooth and creamy.
- Gradually add the confectioners' sugar, mixing on low speed until fully incorporated.
- Mix in the vanilla extract and brewed espresso until smooth and well combined.

6. Assemble the Cake:

- Once the cakes are completely cool, place one cake layer on a serving plate or cake stand.
- Brush the top of the first layer with some of the coffee syrup.
- Spread a layer of mascarpone frosting over the first cake layer.
- Place the second cake layer on top and brush with the remaining coffee syrup.
- Frost the top and sides of the cake with the remaining mascarpone frosting.

7. Decorate:

- Garnish with a dusting of unsweetened cocoa powder and chocolate shavings or grated chocolate if desired.

8. Serve:

- Slice and enjoy your decadent Tiramisu Cake!

This Tiramisu Cake offers a delightful twist on the classic tiramisu, with rich coffee and mascarpone flavors layered into a moist cake. Enjoy!

Salted Caramel Cake

Ingredients:

For the Cake:

- 2 ½ cups (315g) all-purpose flour
- 2 tsp baking powder
- ½ tsp baking soda
- ½ tsp salt
- ½ cup (115g) unsalted butter, softened
- 1 cup (200g) granulated sugar
- ½ cup (100g) packed light brown sugar
- 3 large eggs
- 1 cup (240ml) buttermilk (or whole milk)
- 1 tsp vanilla extract

For the Salted Caramel Sauce:

- 1 cup (200g) granulated sugar
- 6 tbsp (85g) unsalted butter, cut into pieces
- ½ cup (120ml) heavy cream
- 1 tsp sea salt (or to taste)

For the Salted Caramel Frosting:

- ½ cup (115g) unsalted butter, softened
- ½ cup (120g) caramel sauce (homemade or store-bought)
- 2 cups (250g) confectioners' sugar
- 1-2 tbsp milk or heavy cream (to adjust consistency)
- ½ tsp vanilla extract
- Additional sea salt for sprinkling (optional)

For Decoration (Optional):

- Extra caramel sauce
- Sea salt flakes
- Chopped nuts (such as pecans or walnuts)

Instructions:

1. Prepare the Caramel Sauce:

- In a medium saucepan over medium heat, melt the granulated sugar, stirring constantly until it becomes a deep amber color.
- Add the butter, stirring until melted and combined.

- Slowly add the heavy cream while stirring. Be careful, as the mixture will bubble up.
- Stir until smooth and combined. Remove from heat and stir in the sea salt.
- Let the caramel sauce cool to room temperature before using.

2. Preheat the Oven:

- Preheat your oven to 350°F (175°C). Grease and flour two 9-inch round cake pans or line them with parchment paper.

3. Prepare the Cake Batter:

- In a medium bowl, whisk together the flour, baking powder, baking soda, and salt.
- In a large mixing bowl, cream the softened butter, granulated sugar, and brown sugar together until light and fluffy.
- Add the eggs one at a time, beating well after each addition.
- Mix in the vanilla extract.
- Gradually add the dry ingredients to the butter mixture, alternating with the buttermilk. Begin and end with the dry ingredients. Mix until just combined.

4. Bake the Cake:

- Divide the batter evenly between the prepared pans and smooth the tops.
- Bake for 25-30 minutes, or until a toothpick inserted into the center comes out clean.
- Allow the cakes to cool in the pans for 10 minutes, then turn them out onto a wire rack to cool completely.

5. Prepare the Salted Caramel Frosting:

- In a large mixing bowl, beat the softened butter until creamy.
- Gradually add the confectioners' sugar, mixing on low speed until combined.
- Mix in the caramel sauce, vanilla extract, and 1-2 tablespoons of milk or heavy cream until the frosting is smooth and spreadable. Adjust the consistency with more milk if needed.

6. Assemble the Cake:

- Once the cakes are completely cool, place one cake layer on a serving plate or cake stand.
- Spread a layer of salted caramel frosting on top.
- Place the second cake layer on top and frost the top and sides of the cake with the remaining salted caramel frosting.

7. Decorate:

- Drizzle extra caramel sauce over the top of the cake.
- Sprinkle with additional sea salt flakes and chopped nuts if desired.

8. Serve:

- Slice and enjoy your rich and indulgent Salted Caramel Cake!

This Salted Caramel Cake combines moist layers of cake with luscious caramel flavors and a touch of sea salt, making it a delightful treat for any occasion. Enjoy!

Mint Chocolate Cake

Ingredients:

For the Chocolate Cake Layers:

- 1 ¾ cups (220g) all-purpose flour
- 1 ¾ cups (350g) granulated sugar
- ¾ cup (65g) unsweetened cocoa powder
- 1 ½ tsp baking powder
- 1 ½ tsp baking soda
- ½ tsp salt
- 1 cup (240ml) buttermilk (or whole milk)
- ½ cup (120ml) vegetable oil
- 2 large eggs
- 2 tsp vanilla extract
- 1 cup (240ml) boiling water

For the Mint Chocolate Frosting:

- 1 cup (225g) unsalted butter, softened
- 1 ¾ cups (220g) confectioners' sugar
- ½ cup (45g) unsweetened cocoa powder
- 2 tbsp heavy cream (or milk)
- 1 tsp peppermint extract
- A few drops of green food coloring (optional, for color)

For the Mint Ganache:

- ½ cup (120ml) heavy cream
- 1 cup (170g) semisweet chocolate chips
- ½ tsp peppermint extract

For Decoration (Optional):

- Fresh mint leaves
- Chocolate shavings or grated chocolate

Instructions:

1. Preheat the Oven:

- Preheat your oven to 350°F (175°C). Grease and flour two 9-inch round cake pans or line them with parchment paper.

2. Prepare the Chocolate Cake Layers:

- In a large bowl, whisk together the flour, granulated sugar, cocoa powder, baking powder, baking soda, and salt.
- In another bowl, mix the buttermilk, vegetable oil, eggs, and vanilla extract.
- Gradually add the wet ingredients to the dry ingredients, mixing until just combined.
- Stir in the boiling water until the batter is smooth (it will be thin).
- Divide the batter evenly between the prepared pans.
- Bake for 30-35 minutes, or until a toothpick inserted into the center comes out clean.
- Allow the cakes to cool in the pans for 10 minutes, then turn them out onto a wire rack to cool completely.

3. Prepare the Mint Chocolate Frosting:

- In a large mixing bowl, beat the softened butter until creamy.
- Gradually add the confectioners' sugar and cocoa powder, mixing on low speed until combined.
- Add the heavy cream, peppermint extract, and a few drops of green food coloring if using. Beat until smooth and fluffy.

4. Prepare the Mint Ganache:

- In a small saucepan, heat the heavy cream over medium heat until it just begins to simmer.
- Remove from heat and add the chocolate chips. Let sit for 2 minutes, then stir until smooth.
- Stir in the peppermint extract. Let the ganache cool slightly before using.

5. Assemble the Cake:

- Once the cakes are completely cool, place one cake layer on a serving plate or cake stand.
- Spread a layer of mint chocolate frosting on top.
- Place the second cake layer on top and frost the top and sides of the cake with the remaining mint chocolate frosting.

6. Add the Mint Ganache:

- Pour the mint ganache over the top of the cake, allowing it to drip down the sides.

7. Decorate (Optional):

- Garnish with fresh mint leaves and chocolate shavings or grated chocolate if desired.

8. Serve:

- Slice and enjoy your delicious Mint Chocolate Cake!

This Mint Chocolate Cake combines the rich flavors of chocolate with a refreshing hint of mint, creating a delightful dessert that's sure to impress. Enjoy!

Apple Cinnamon Cake

Ingredients:

For the Cake:

- 1 ½ cups (190g) all-purpose flour
- 1 tsp baking powder
- ½ tsp baking soda
- ½ tsp salt
- 1 tsp ground cinnamon
- ½ tsp ground nutmeg
- ½ cup (115g) unsalted butter, softened
- 1 cup (200g) granulated sugar
- 2 large eggs
- 1 cup (240ml) buttermilk (or whole milk)
- 1 tsp vanilla extract
- 1 ½ cups (about 2 medium) peeled and diced apples (such as Granny Smith or Honeycrisp)

For the Cinnamon Sugar Swirl:

- ¼ cup (50g) granulated sugar
- 1 tsp ground cinnamon

For the Apple Cinnamon Glaze (Optional):

- 1 cup (125g) confectioners' sugar
- 2 tbsp milk
- ½ tsp vanilla extract
- ¼ tsp ground cinnamon

For Decoration (Optional):

- Additional ground cinnamon
- Sliced apples

Instructions:

1. Preheat the Oven:

- Preheat your oven to 350°F (175°C). Grease and flour a 9-inch round cake pan or line it with parchment paper.

2. Prepare the Cake Batter:

- In a medium bowl, whisk together the flour, baking powder, baking soda, salt, cinnamon, and nutmeg.
- In a large mixing bowl, cream the softened butter and granulated sugar together until light and fluffy.
- Add the eggs one at a time, beating well after each addition.
- Mix in the vanilla extract.
- Gradually add the dry ingredients to the butter mixture, alternating with the buttermilk. Begin and end with the dry ingredients. Mix until just combined.
- Gently fold in the diced apples.

3. Prepare the Cinnamon Sugar Swirl:

- In a small bowl, mix together the granulated sugar and ground cinnamon.

4. Assemble the Cake:

- Pour half of the cake batter into the prepared pan and smooth the top.
- Sprinkle half of the cinnamon sugar mixture over the batter.
- Add the remaining cake batter on top and smooth it out.
- Sprinkle the remaining cinnamon sugar mixture over the top of the cake.

5. Bake the Cake:

- Bake for 35-40 minutes, or until a toothpick inserted into the center comes out clean.
- Allow the cake to cool in the pan for 10 minutes, then turn it out onto a wire rack to cool completely.

6. Prepare the Apple Cinnamon Glaze (Optional):

- In a small bowl, whisk together the confectioners' sugar, milk, vanilla extract, and ground cinnamon until smooth. Adjust the consistency with more milk if needed.

7. Decorate the Cake:

- If using, drizzle the apple cinnamon glaze over the cooled cake.
- Garnish with a dusting of ground cinnamon and sliced apples if desired.

8. Serve:

- Slice and enjoy your warm, flavorful Apple Cinnamon Cake!

This Apple Cinnamon Cake is wonderfully spiced and packed with tender apple chunks, making it a comforting and delicious treat. Enjoy with a cup of tea or coffee!

Chocolate Hazelnut Cake

Ingredients:

For the Cake:

- 1 ½ cups all-purpose flour
- 1 cup granulated sugar
- ¾ cup unsweetened cocoa powder
- 1 tsp baking powder
- 1 tsp baking soda
- ½ tsp salt
- ½ cup finely ground hazelnuts (about 70g)
- 2 large eggs
- 1 cup buttermilk
- ½ cup vegetable oil
- 1 tsp vanilla extract
- 1 cup hot water

For the Hazelnut Praline (Optional):

- ½ cup sugar
- ¼ cup water
- 1 cup whole hazelnuts (toasted and skinned)

For the Frosting:

- 1 cup unsalted butter, room temperature
- 3 cups powdered sugar
- ½ cup unsweetened cocoa powder
- ¼ cup heavy cream (more if needed)
- 1 tsp vanilla extract
- Pinch of salt

Instructions:

1. Prepare the Cake:

   1. Preheat Oven: Preheat your oven to 350°F (175°C). Grease and flour two 9-inch round cake pans or line them with parchment paper.
   2. Mix Dry Ingredients: In a large bowl, whisk together the flour, sugar, cocoa powder, baking powder, baking soda, salt, and ground hazelnuts.
   3. Combine Wet Ingredients: In another bowl, beat the eggs. Then mix in the buttermilk, vegetable oil, and vanilla extract.

4. Combine Mixtures: Add the wet ingredients to the dry ingredients and mix until just combined. Gradually stir in the hot water until the batter is smooth (the batter will be thin).
5. Bake: Divide the batter evenly between the prepared pans. Bake for 30-35 minutes, or until a toothpick inserted into the center comes out clean. Let the cakes cool in the pans for 10 minutes, then transfer to a wire rack to cool completely.

2. Prepare the Hazelnut Praline (Optional):

1. Cook Sugar: In a medium saucepan, combine sugar and water. Cook over medium heat, without stirring, until the mixture turns a deep amber color.
2. Add Hazelnuts: Quickly stir in the toasted hazelnuts and pour the mixture onto a parchment-lined baking sheet. Allow it to cool completely. Once hardened, break it into pieces and process in a food processor until it becomes a coarse powder.

3. Prepare the Frosting:

1. Beat Butter: In a large bowl, beat the butter with an electric mixer until creamy.
2. Add Sugar and Cocoa: Gradually add powdered sugar and cocoa powder, beating on low speed until combined.
3. Add Cream and Vanilla: Add heavy cream, vanilla extract, and a pinch of salt. Beat on high speed until the frosting is light and fluffy. Adjust the consistency by adding more cream if needed.

4. Assemble the Cake:

1. Level Cakes: If necessary, level the tops of the cooled cakes with a knife or cake leveler.
2. Frost: Place one cake layer on a serving plate or cake stand. Spread a layer of frosting on top. Place the second layer on top and frost the top and sides of the cake.
3. Decorate: Optionally, sprinkle the top with crushed hazelnut praline or chopped hazelnuts for extra texture and flavor.

Enjoy your homemade Chocolate Hazelnut Cake! It's rich, moist, and has a delightful nutty flavor that's sure to impress.

Key Lime Cake

Ingredients:

For the Cake:

- 2 ¼ cups (280g) all-purpose flour
- 1 ½ tsp baking powder
- ½ tsp baking soda
- ¼ tsp salt
- ½ cup (115g) unsalted butter, softened
- 1 cup (200g) granulated sugar
- 3 large eggs
- 1 cup (240ml) buttermilk (or whole milk)
- ½ cup (120ml) fresh lime juice (about 3-4 limes)
- 2 tbsp lime zest
- 1 tsp vanilla extract

For the Key Lime Frosting:

- 1 cup (225g) unsalted butter, softened
- 4 cups (500g) confectioners' sugar
- ¼ cup (60ml) fresh lime juice
- 1 tbsp lime zest
- 1 tsp vanilla extract
- A pinch of salt

For Decoration (Optional):

- Additional lime zest
- Lime slices
- Whipped cream

Instructions:

1. Preheat the Oven:

- Preheat your oven to 350°F (175°C). Grease and flour two 9-inch round cake pans or line them with parchment paper.

2. Prepare the Cake Batter:

- In a medium bowl, whisk together the flour, baking powder, baking soda, and salt.
- In a large bowl, cream the softened butter and granulated sugar until light and fluffy.
- Add the eggs one at a time, beating well after each addition.
- Mix in the vanilla extract.

- Gradually add the dry ingredients to the butter mixture, alternating with the buttermilk. Begin and end with the dry ingredients. Mix until just combined.
- Fold in the lime juice and lime zest.

3. Bake the Cake:

- Divide the batter evenly between the prepared pans and smooth the tops.
- Bake for 25-30 minutes, or until a toothpick inserted into the center comes out clean.
- Allow the cakes to cool in the pans for 10 minutes, then turn them out onto a wire rack to cool completely.

4. Prepare the Key Lime Frosting:

- In a large mixing bowl, beat the softened butter until creamy.
- Gradually add the confectioners' sugar, mixing on low speed until combined.
- Mix in the lime juice, lime zest, vanilla extract, and a pinch of salt until smooth and fluffy.

5. Assemble the Cake:

- Once the cakes are completely cool, place one cake layer on a serving plate or cake stand.
- Spread a layer of key lime frosting on top.
- Place the second cake layer on top and frost the top and sides with the remaining key lime frosting.

6. Decorate (Optional):

- Garnish with additional lime zest, lime slices, and whipped cream if desired.

7. Serve:

- Slice and enjoy your tangy and refreshing Key Lime Cake!

Both of these cakes offer distinct and delightful flavors, perfect for a variety of occasions. Enjoy baking and indulging in these delicious treats!

Almond Cake with Raspberry Filling

Ingredients:

For the Almond Cake:

- 1 ¼ cups (155g) all-purpose flour
- 1 ¼ cups (125g) almond flour (or finely ground almonds)
- 1 ½ tsp baking powder
- ¼ tsp salt
- ½ cup (115g) unsalted butter, softened
- 1 cup (200g) granulated sugar
- 3 large eggs
- 1 tsp vanilla extract
- ¼ tsp almond extract
- ½ cup (120ml) milk (or buttermilk)
- ¼ cup (60ml) sour cream

For the Raspberry Filling:

- 1 ½ cups (180g) fresh or frozen raspberries
- ¼ cup (50g) granulated sugar
- 1 tbsp lemon juice
- 1 tbsp cornstarch mixed with 1 tbsp water (optional, for thickening)

For the Almond Buttercream Frosting:

- 1 cup (225g) unsalted butter, softened
- 3 ½ cups (440g) confectioners' sugar
- 1 tsp vanilla extract
- ¼ tsp almond extract
- 2-3 tbsp milk (to adjust consistency)

For Decoration (Optional):

- Sliced almonds
- Fresh raspberries

Instructions:

1. Prepare the Raspberry Filling:

- In a medium saucepan, combine the raspberries, granulated sugar, and lemon juice. Cook over medium heat, stirring occasionally, until the raspberries break down and the mixture starts to thicken (about 5-7 minutes).

- If the filling is too runny, stir in the cornstarch-water mixture and cook for an additional 1-2 minutes until thickened.
- Remove from heat and let cool completely.

2. Preheat the Oven:

- Preheat your oven to 350°F (175°C). Grease and flour two 9-inch round cake pans or line them with parchment paper.

3. Prepare the Almond Cake Batter:

- In a medium bowl, whisk together the all-purpose flour, almond flour, baking powder, and salt.
- In a large mixing bowl, cream the softened butter and granulated sugar until light and fluffy.
- Add the eggs one at a time, beating well after each addition.
- Mix in the vanilla and almond extracts.
- Gradually add the dry ingredients to the butter mixture, alternating with the milk and sour cream. Begin and end with the dry ingredients. Mix until just combined.

4. Bake the Cake:

- Divide the batter evenly between the prepared pans and smooth the tops.
- Bake for 25-30 minutes, or until a toothpick inserted into the center comes out clean.
- Allow the cakes to cool in the pans for 10 minutes, then turn them out onto a wire rack to cool completely.

5. Prepare the Almond Buttercream Frosting:

- In a large mixing bowl, beat the softened butter until creamy.
- Gradually add the confectioners' sugar, mixing on low speed until combined.
- Mix in the vanilla extract, almond extract, and 2-3 tablespoons of milk until smooth and spreadable. Adjust the consistency with more milk if needed.

6. Assemble the Cake:

- Once the cakes are completely cool, place one cake layer on a serving plate or cake stand.
- Spread the cooled raspberry filling evenly over the top of the first cake layer.
- Place the second cake layer on top of the raspberry filling.
- Frost the top and sides of the cake with the almond buttercream frosting.

7. Decorate (Optional):

- Garnish with sliced almonds and fresh raspberries for a decorative touch.

8. Serve:

- Slice and enjoy your delicious Almond Cake with Raspberry Filling!

This Almond Cake with Raspberry Filling combines the nutty flavor of almonds with the tartness of raspberries, making it a delightful and elegant dessert. Enjoy!

Gingerbread Cake

Ingredients:

For the Cake:

- 2 ¼ cups (280g) all-purpose flour
- 1 ½ tsp ground ginger
- 1 ½ tsp ground cinnamon
- ¼ tsp ground cloves
- ¼ tsp ground nutmeg
- 1 tsp baking soda
- ¼ tsp salt
- ½ cup (115g) unsalted butter, softened
- ½ cup (100g) granulated sugar
- ½ cup (100g) packed light brown sugar
- 2 large eggs
- 1 cup (240ml) molasses (preferably unsulfured)
- 1 cup (240ml) hot water
- 1 tsp vanilla extract

For the Cream Cheese Frosting (Optional):

- 8 oz (225g) cream cheese, softened
- ½ cup (115g) unsalted butter, softened
- 4 cups (500g) confectioners' sugar
- 1 tsp vanilla extract
- A pinch of salt

For Decoration (Optional):

- Ground cinnamon
- Freshly grated nutmeg
- Crystallized ginger pieces

Instructions:

1. Preheat the Oven:

- Preheat your oven to 350°F (175°C). Grease and flour a 9x13-inch baking pan or two 9-inch round cake pans. You can also line the pans with parchment paper for easier removal.

2. Prepare the Cake Batter:

- In a medium bowl, whisk together the flour, ginger, cinnamon, cloves, nutmeg, baking soda, and salt.
- In a large mixing bowl, cream the softened butter, granulated sugar, and brown sugar until light and fluffy.
- Add the eggs one at a time, beating well after each addition.
- Mix in the molasses and vanilla extract until well combined.
- Gradually add the dry ingredients to the butter mixture, alternating with the hot water. Begin and end with the dry ingredients. Mix until just combined.

3. Bake the Cake:

- Pour the batter into the prepared pan(s) and smooth the top.
- Bake for 30-35 minutes, or until a toothpick inserted into the center comes out clean.
- Allow the cake to cool in the pan for 10 minutes, then turn it out onto a wire rack to cool completely.

4. Prepare the Cream Cheese Frosting (Optional):

- In a large mixing bowl, beat the softened cream cheese and butter together until smooth and creamy.
- Gradually add the confectioners' sugar, mixing on low speed until fully incorporated.
- Mix in the vanilla extract and a pinch of salt until smooth and fluffy.

5. Frost and Decorate the Cake (Optional):

- Once the cake is completely cool, frost with the cream cheese frosting.
- Garnish with a sprinkle of ground cinnamon, freshly grated nutmeg, and/or crystallized ginger pieces if desired.

6. Serve:

- Slice and enjoy your spiced, moist Gingerbread Cake!

This Gingerbread Cake is rich with warm spices and has a lovely depth of flavor from the molasses. It's perfect on its own or with a dollop of cream cheese frosting. Enjoy!

Maple Pecan Cake

Ingredients:

For the Cake:

- 1 ¾ cups (220g) all-purpose flour
- 1 ½ tsp baking powder
- ½ tsp baking soda
- ¼ tsp salt
- ½ cup (115g) unsalted butter, softened
- 1 cup (200g) granulated sugar
- ½ cup (100g) packed light brown sugar
- 2 large eggs
- 1 cup (240ml) pure maple syrup
- ½ cup (120ml) buttermilk (or whole milk)
- 1 tsp vanilla extract
- 1 cup (120g) chopped pecans (toasted if desired)

For the Maple Pecan Frosting:

- 1 cup (225g) unsalted butter, softened
- 3 ½ cups (440g) confectioners' sugar
- ¼ cup (60ml) pure maple syrup
- 2-3 tbsp milk or heavy cream (to adjust consistency)
- 1 tsp vanilla extract
- ½ cup (60g) chopped pecans (for decoration)

For Decoration (Optional):

- Additional pecans
- Drizzle of pure maple syrup

Instructions:

1. Preheat the Oven:

- Preheat your oven to 350°F (175°C). Grease and flour two 9-inch round cake pans or line them with parchment paper.

2. Prepare the Cake Batter:

- In a medium bowl, whisk together the flour, baking powder, baking soda, and salt.
- In a large mixing bowl, cream the softened butter, granulated sugar, and brown sugar until light and fluffy.
- Add the eggs one at a time, beating well after each addition.

- Mix in the vanilla extract.
- Gradually add the dry ingredients to the butter mixture, alternating with the maple syrup and buttermilk. Begin and end with the dry ingredients. Mix until just combined.
- Fold in the chopped pecans.

3. Bake the Cake:

- Divide the batter evenly between the prepared pans and smooth the tops.
- Bake for 25-30 minutes, or until a toothpick inserted into the center comes out clean.
- Allow the cakes to cool in the pans for 10 minutes, then turn them out onto a wire rack to cool completely.

4. Prepare the Maple Pecan Frosting:

- In a large mixing bowl, beat the softened butter until creamy.
- Gradually add the confectioners' sugar, mixing on low speed until combined.
- Mix in the maple syrup, vanilla extract, and 2-3 tablespoons of milk or heavy cream until smooth and spreadable. Adjust the consistency with more milk if needed.

5. Assemble the Cake:

- Once the cakes are completely cool, place one cake layer on a serving plate or cake stand.
- Spread a layer of maple pecan frosting on top.
- Place the second cake layer on top and frost the top and sides with the remaining maple pecan frosting.

6. Decorate (Optional):

- Garnish with additional chopped pecans and a drizzle of pure maple syrup if desired.

7. Serve:

- Slice and enjoy your delectable Maple Pecan Cake!

This Maple Pecan Cake is a perfect blend of sweet maple syrup and crunchy pecans, making it a delightful treat for any occasion. Enjoy!

Orange Blossom Cake

Ingredients:

For the Cake:

- 2 ½ cups (315g) all-purpose flour
- 1 ½ tsp baking powder
- ½ tsp baking soda
- ¼ tsp salt
- ½ cup (115g) unsalted butter, softened
- 1 cup (200g) granulated sugar
- ½ cup (100g) light brown sugar
- 3 large eggs
- 1 cup (240ml) buttermilk (or whole milk)
- ½ cup (120ml) fresh orange juice
- 2 tbsp orange zest (from about 2 oranges)
- 1 tsp orange blossom water (available at specialty stores or online)
- 1 tsp vanilla extract

For the Orange Blossom Frosting:

- 1 cup (225g) unsalted butter, softened
- 4 cups (500g) confectioners' sugar
- ¼ cup (60ml) fresh orange juice
- 1 tsp orange blossom water
- 1 tsp vanilla extract
- A pinch of salt

For Decoration (Optional):

- Candied orange slices
- Fresh edible flowers
- Orange zest

Instructions:

1. Preheat the Oven:

- Preheat your oven to 350°F (175°C). Grease and flour two 9-inch round cake pans or line them with parchment paper.

2. Prepare the Cake Batter:

- In a medium bowl, whisk together the flour, baking powder, baking soda, and salt.

- In a large mixing bowl, cream the softened butter, granulated sugar, and light brown sugar until light and fluffy.
- Add the eggs one at a time, beating well after each addition.
- Mix in the vanilla extract and orange blossom water.
- Gradually add the dry ingredients to the butter mixture, alternating with the buttermilk and fresh orange juice. Begin and end with the dry ingredients. Mix until just combined.
- Fold in the orange zest.

3. Bake the Cake:

- Divide the batter evenly between the prepared pans and smooth the tops.
- Bake for 25-30 minutes, or until a toothpick inserted into the center comes out clean.
- Allow the cakes to cool in the pans for 10 minutes, then turn them out onto a wire rack to cool completely.

4. Prepare the Orange Blossom Frosting:

- In a large mixing bowl, beat the softened butter until creamy.
- Gradually add the confectioners' sugar, mixing on low speed until fully incorporated.
- Mix in the fresh orange juice, orange blossom water, vanilla extract, and a pinch of salt until smooth and fluffy. Adjust the consistency with more orange juice or confectioners' sugar if needed.

5. Assemble the Cake:

- Once the cakes are completely cool, place one cake layer on a serving plate or cake stand.
- Spread a layer of orange blossom frosting on top.
- Place the second cake layer on top and frost the top and sides with the remaining orange blossom frosting.

6. Decorate (Optional):

- Garnish with candied orange slices, fresh edible flowers, and additional orange zest if desired.

7. Serve:

- Slice and enjoy your fragrant and elegant Orange Blossom Cake!

This Orange Blossom Cake is light and fragrant with a lovely citrus flavor, perfect for a special occasion or a delightful treat. Enjoy!

Matcha Green Tea Cake

Ingredients:

For the Cake:

- 1 ½ cups (190g) all-purpose flour
- 1 ½ tsp baking powder
- ½ tsp baking soda
- ¼ tsp salt
- 2 tbsp matcha green tea powder (ceremonial grade preferred)
- ½ cup (115g) unsalted butter, softened
- 1 cup (200g) granulated sugar
- 3 large eggs
- 1 cup (240ml) buttermilk (or whole milk)
- 1 tsp vanilla extract

For the Matcha Frosting:

- 1 cup (225g) unsalted butter, softened
- 3 ½ cups (440g) confectioners' sugar
- 2 tbsp matcha green tea powder
- 2-3 tbsp milk or heavy cream (to adjust consistency)
- 1 tsp vanilla extract
- A pinch of salt

For Decoration (Optional):

- Additional matcha powder
- Edible flowers
- Fresh berries

Instructions:

1. Preheat the Oven:

- Preheat your oven to 350°F (175°C). Grease and flour two 9-inch round cake pans or line them with parchment paper.

2. Prepare the Cake Batter:

- In a medium bowl, whisk together the flour, baking powder, baking soda, salt, and matcha green tea powder.
- In a large mixing bowl, cream the softened butter and granulated sugar until light and fluffy.
- Add the eggs one at a time, beating well after each addition.

- Mix in the vanilla extract.
- Gradually add the dry ingredients to the butter mixture, alternating with the buttermilk. Begin and end with the dry ingredients. Mix until just combined.

3. Bake the Cake:

- Divide the batter evenly between the prepared pans and smooth the tops.
- Bake for 25-30 minutes, or until a toothpick inserted into the center comes out clean.
- Allow the cakes to cool in the pans for 10 minutes, then turn them out onto a wire rack to cool completely.

4. Prepare the Matcha Frosting:

- In a large mixing bowl, beat the softened butter until creamy.
- Gradually add the confectioners' sugar, mixing on low speed until combined.
- Mix in the matcha green tea powder, vanilla extract, and a pinch of salt until well combined.
- Add 2-3 tablespoons of milk or heavy cream to achieve a smooth, spreadable consistency. Adjust as needed.

5. Assemble the Cake:

- Once the cakes are completely cool, place one cake layer on a serving plate or cake stand.
- Spread a layer of matcha frosting on top.
- Place the second cake layer on top and frost the top and sides with the remaining matcha frosting.

6. Decorate (Optional):

- Garnish with a light dusting of matcha powder, edible flowers, and fresh berries if desired.

7. Serve:

- Slice and enjoy your elegant and flavorful Matcha Green Tea Cake!

This cake is a beautiful balance of subtle matcha flavor and sweetness, making it a sophisticated treat for any occasion. Enjoy!

White Chocolate and Raspberry Cake

Ingredients:

For the Cake:

- 2 ½ cups (315g) all-purpose flour
- 1 ½ tsp baking powder
- ½ tsp baking soda
- ¼ tsp salt
- ½ cup (115g) unsalted butter, softened
- 1 cup (200g) granulated sugar
- ½ cup (100g) packed light brown sugar
- 3 large eggs
- 1 cup (240ml) buttermilk (or whole milk)
- 1 tsp vanilla extract
- 1 cup (170g) white chocolate chips or finely chopped white chocolate
- 1 cup (120g) fresh raspberries (or frozen, thawed and drained)

For the White Chocolate Raspberry Frosting:

- 8 oz (225g) cream cheese, softened
- ½ cup (115g) unsalted butter, softened
- 2 cups (250g) confectioners' sugar
- 4 oz (115g) white chocolate, melted and cooled
- 1 tsp vanilla extract
- ¼ cup (60ml) heavy cream (or milk)

For Decoration (Optional):

- Fresh raspberries
- White chocolate shavings
- Mint leaves

Instructions:

1. Preheat the Oven:

- Preheat your oven to 350°F (175°C). Grease and flour two 9-inch round cake pans or line them with parchment paper.

2. Prepare the Cake Batter:

- In a medium bowl, whisk together the flour, baking powder, baking soda, and salt.
- In a large mixing bowl, cream the softened butter, granulated sugar, and brown sugar until light and fluffy.

- Add the eggs one at a time, beating well after each addition.
- Mix in the vanilla extract.
- Gradually add the dry ingredients to the butter mixture, alternating with the buttermilk. Begin and end with the dry ingredients. Mix until just combined.
- Fold in the white chocolate chips and fresh raspberries.

3. Bake the Cake:

- Divide the batter evenly between the prepared pans and smooth the tops.
- Bake for 25-30 minutes, or until a toothpick inserted into the center comes out clean.
- Allow the cakes to cool in the pans for 10 minutes, then turn them out onto a wire rack to cool completely.

4. Prepare the White Chocolate Raspberry Frosting:

- In a large mixing bowl, beat the softened cream cheese and butter until creamy.
- Gradually add the confectioners' sugar, mixing on low speed until fully incorporated.
- Mix in the melted white chocolate and vanilla extract until smooth.
- Add the heavy cream (or milk) and beat until the frosting is light and fluffy.

5. Assemble the Cake:

- Once the cakes are completely cool, place one cake layer on a serving plate or cake stand.
- Spread a layer of white chocolate raspberry frosting on top.
- Place the second cake layer on top and frost the top and sides with the remaining frosting.

6. Decorate (Optional):

- Garnish with fresh raspberries, white chocolate shavings, and mint leaves if desired.

7. Serve:

- Slice and enjoy your rich and fruity White Chocolate and Raspberry Cake!

This cake offers a wonderful combination of creamy white chocolate and tart raspberries, making it a perfect treat for special occasions or a delightful dessert anytime. Enjoy!

Toffee Cake

Ingredients:

For the Cake:

- 1 ¾ cups (220g) all-purpose flour
- 1 ½ tsp baking powder
- ½ tsp baking soda
- ¼ tsp salt
- ½ cup (115g) unsalted butter, softened
- 1 cup (200g) granulated sugar
- ½ cup (100g) packed light brown sugar
- 2 large eggs
- 1 cup (240ml) buttermilk (or whole milk)
- 1 tsp vanilla extract
- ½ cup (120ml) toffee sauce (store-bought or homemade, see below)

For the Toffee Sauce (Optional but recommended for extra flavor):

- 1 cup (200g) packed light brown sugar
- ½ cup (115g) unsalted butter
- ¼ cup (60ml) heavy cream
- 1 tsp vanilla extract
- A pinch of salt

For the Toffee Frosting:

- 1 cup (225g) unsalted butter, softened
- 3 ½ cups (440g) confectioners' sugar
- ¼ cup (60ml) heavy cream (or milk)
- ¼ cup (60ml) toffee sauce (store-bought or homemade)
- 1 tsp vanilla extract
- A pinch of salt

For Decoration (Optional):

- Crumbled toffee pieces or bits
- Additional toffee sauce for drizzling

Instructions:

1. Prepare the Toffee Sauce (Optional):

- In a medium saucepan, combine the brown sugar, butter, and heavy cream.

- Cook over medium heat, stirring constantly, until the sugar is dissolved and the mixture is smooth.
- Bring to a gentle boil and cook for 2-3 minutes until slightly thickened.
- Remove from heat and stir in the vanilla extract and a pinch of salt. Let it cool to room temperature.

2. Preheat the Oven:

- Preheat your oven to 350°F (175°C). Grease and flour two 9-inch round cake pans or line them with parchment paper.

3. Prepare the Cake Batter:

- In a medium bowl, whisk together the flour, baking powder, baking soda, and salt.
- In a large mixing bowl, cream the softened butter, granulated sugar, and brown sugar until light and fluffy.
- Add the eggs one at a time, beating well after each addition.
- Mix in the vanilla extract.
- Gradually add the dry ingredients to the butter mixture, alternating with the buttermilk. Begin and end with the dry ingredients. Mix until just combined.
- Stir in the ½ cup of toffee sauce.

4. Bake the Cake:

- Divide the batter evenly between the prepared pans and smooth the tops.
- Bake for 25-30 minutes, or until a toothpick inserted into the center comes out clean.
- Allow the cakes to cool in the pans for 10 minutes, then turn them out onto a wire rack to cool completely.

5. Prepare the Toffee Frosting:

- In a large mixing bowl, beat the softened butter until creamy.
- Gradually add the confectioners' sugar, mixing on low speed until fully incorporated.
- Mix in the heavy cream, toffee sauce, vanilla extract, and a pinch of salt until smooth and fluffy. Adjust consistency with more cream or confectioners' sugar as needed.

6. Assemble the Cake:

- Once the cakes are completely cool, place one cake layer on a serving plate or cake stand.
- Spread a layer of toffee frosting on top.
- Place the second cake layer on top and frost the top and sides with the remaining toffee frosting.

7. Decorate (Optional):

- Garnish with crumbled toffee pieces or bits and drizzle additional toffee sauce over the top.

8. Serve:

- Slice and enjoy your decadent Toffee Cake!

This Toffee Cake is rich and buttery with a sweet toffee flavor that pairs wonderfully with the creamy toffee frosting. It's perfect for a special treat or any celebration. Enjoy!

Fig and Walnut Cake

Ingredients:

For the Cake:

- 1 ½ cups (190g) all-purpose flour
- 1 tsp baking powder
- ½ tsp baking soda
- ¼ tsp salt
- ½ tsp ground cinnamon
- ½ tsp ground nutmeg
- ½ cup (115g) unsalted butter, softened
- ¾ cup (150g) granulated sugar
- ¼ cup (50g) packed light brown sugar
- 2 large eggs
- ½ cup (120ml) buttermilk (or whole milk)
- 1 tsp vanilla extract
- 1 cup (200g) dried figs, chopped
- ¾ cup (90g) chopped walnuts (toasted if desired)

For the Fig Glaze (Optional):

- ½ cup (120ml) fig jam or preserves
- 2 tbsp water

For Decoration (Optional):

- Whole figs (fresh or dried)
- Additional chopped walnuts
- Powdered sugar

Instructions:

1. Preheat the Oven:

- Preheat your oven to 350°F (175°C). Grease and flour a 9-inch round cake pan or line it with parchment paper.

2. Prepare the Cake Batter:

- In a medium bowl, whisk together the flour, baking powder, baking soda, salt, cinnamon, and nutmeg.
- In a large mixing bowl, cream the softened butter, granulated sugar, and brown sugar until light and fluffy.
- Add the eggs one at a time, beating well after each addition.

- Mix in the vanilla extract.
- Gradually add the dry ingredients to the butter mixture, alternating with the buttermilk. Begin and end with the dry ingredients. Mix until just combined.
- Fold in the chopped figs and walnuts.

3. Bake the Cake:

- Pour the batter into the prepared pan and smooth the top.
- Bake for 30-35 minutes, or until a toothpick inserted into the center comes out clean.
- Allow the cake to cool in the pan for 10 minutes, then turn it out onto a wire rack to cool completely.

4. Prepare the Fig Glaze (Optional):

- In a small saucepan, combine the fig jam and water.
- Heat over low heat, stirring until the mixture is smooth and slightly thinned out.
- Allow it to cool slightly before using.

5. Frost and Decorate:

- Once the cake is completely cool, you can brush it with the fig glaze if desired.
- Garnish with whole figs, additional chopped walnuts, and a dusting of powdered sugar if you like.

6. Serve:

- Slice and enjoy your delicious Fig and Walnut Cake!

This Fig and Walnut Cake has a delightful texture and flavor combination, making it a perfect treat for any occasion. Enjoy!

Cherry Almond Cake

Ingredients:

For the Cake:

- 1 ½ cups (190g) all-purpose flour
- 1 ½ tsp baking powder
- ¼ tsp baking soda
- ¼ tsp salt
- ½ cup (115g) unsalted butter, softened
- 1 cup (200g) granulated sugar
- 2 large eggs
- ½ cup (120ml) sour cream (or plain yogurt)
- 1 tsp vanilla extract
- 1 tsp almond extract
- 1 cup (150g) chopped fresh or frozen cherries (thawed and drained)
- ½ cup (60g) sliced almonds (toasted if desired)

For the Cherry Almond Frosting:

- 8 oz (225g) cream cheese, softened
- ½ cup (115g) unsalted butter, softened
- 3 cups (375g) confectioners' sugar
- 2 tbsp milk or heavy cream
- 1 tsp vanilla extract
- 1 tsp almond extract

For Decoration (Optional):

- Additional sliced almonds
- Fresh cherries
- A dusting of powdered sugar

Instructions:

1. Preheat the Oven:

- Preheat your oven to 350°F (175°C). Grease and flour a 9-inch round cake pan or line it with parchment paper.

2. Prepare the Cake Batter:

- In a medium bowl, whisk together the flour, baking powder, baking soda, and salt.
- In a large mixing bowl, cream the softened butter and granulated sugar until light and fluffy.

- Add the eggs one at a time, beating well after each addition.
- Mix in the vanilla extract and almond extract.
- Gradually add the dry ingredients to the butter mixture, alternating with the sour cream. Begin and end with the dry ingredients. Mix until just combined.
- Gently fold in the chopped cherries and sliced almonds.

3. Bake the Cake:

- Pour the batter into the prepared pan and smooth the top.
- Bake for 25-30 minutes, or until a toothpick inserted into the center comes out clean.
- Allow the cake to cool in the pan for 10 minutes, then turn it out onto a wire rack to cool completely.

4. Prepare the Cherry Almond Frosting:

- In a large mixing bowl, beat the softened cream cheese and butter until creamy.
- Gradually add the confectioners' sugar, mixing on low speed until combined.
- Mix in the milk or heavy cream, vanilla extract, and almond extract until smooth and fluffy.

5. Assemble the Cake:

- Once the cake is completely cool, spread the cherry almond frosting evenly over the top and sides of the cake.

6. Decorate (Optional):

- Garnish with additional sliced almonds, fresh cherries, and a dusting of powdered sugar if desired.

7. Serve:

- Slice and enjoy your delightful Cherry Almond Cake!

This cake offers a wonderful combination of flavors and textures with the sweet cherries and nutty almonds. It's perfect for any celebration or as a special treat for yourself. Enjoy!

Hazelnut Mocha Cake

Ingredients:

For the Cake:

- 1 ¾ cups (220g) all-purpose flour
- 1 ½ tsp baking powder
- ½ tsp baking soda
- ¼ tsp salt
- ¼ cup (25g) unsweetened cocoa powder
- 1 tbsp instant coffee granules (or espresso powder)
- ½ cup (115g) unsalted butter, softened
- 1 cup (200g) granulated sugar
- ½ cup (100g) packed light brown sugar
- 2 large eggs
- ½ cup (120ml) buttermilk (or whole milk)
- ½ cup (120ml) hot brewed coffee
- 1 tsp vanilla extract
- ¾ cup (90g) finely chopped hazelnuts (toasted if desired)

For the Hazelnut Mocha Frosting:

- 1 cup (225g) unsalted butter, softened
- 3 ½ cups (440g) confectioners' sugar
- ¼ cup (25g) unsweetened cocoa powder
- 2 tbsp instant coffee granules (or espresso powder)
- 2-3 tbsp milk or heavy cream (to adjust consistency)
- 1 tsp vanilla extract
- ½ cup (60g) finely chopped hazelnuts (for decoration)

For Decoration (Optional):

- Whole or chopped toasted hazelnuts
- Chocolate shavings or cocoa powder

Instructions:

1. Preheat the Oven:

- Preheat your oven to 350°F (175°C). Grease and flour two 9-inch round cake pans or line them with parchment paper.

2. Prepare the Cake Batter:

- In a medium bowl, whisk together the flour, baking powder, baking soda, salt, cocoa powder, and instant coffee granules.
- In a large mixing bowl, cream the softened butter, granulated sugar, and brown sugar until light and fluffy.
- Add the eggs one at a time, beating well after each addition.
- Mix in the vanilla extract.
- Gradually add the dry ingredients to the butter mixture, alternating with the buttermilk and hot coffee. Begin and end with the dry ingredients. Mix until just combined.
- Fold in the chopped hazelnuts.

3. Bake the Cake:

- Divide the batter evenly between the prepared pans and smooth the tops.
- Bake for 25-30 minutes, or until a toothpick inserted into the center comes out clean.
- Allow the cakes to cool in the pans for 10 minutes, then turn them out onto a wire rack to cool completely.

4. Prepare the Hazelnut Mocha Frosting:

- In a large mixing bowl, beat the softened butter until creamy.
- Gradually add the confectioners' sugar, mixing on low speed until fully incorporated.
- Mix in the cocoa powder, instant coffee granules, and vanilla extract until smooth.
- Add 2-3 tablespoons of milk or heavy cream to achieve a smooth, spreadable consistency. Adjust as needed.

5. Assemble the Cake:

- Once the cakes are completely cool, place one cake layer on a serving plate or cake stand.
- Spread a layer of hazelnut mocha frosting on top.
- Place the second cake layer on top and frost the top and sides with the remaining frosting.

6. Decorate (Optional):

- Garnish with whole or chopped toasted hazelnuts and chocolate shavings or a dusting of cocoa powder if desired.

7. Serve:

- Slice and enjoy your rich and flavorful Hazelnut Mocha Cake!

This cake is a delightful combination of chocolate, coffee, and hazelnut flavors, making it a perfect treat for any coffee or chocolate lover. Enjoy!

Pear and Ginger Cake

Ingredients:

For the Cake:

- 1 ½ cups (190g) all-purpose flour
- 1 tsp baking powder
- ½ tsp baking soda
- ¼ tsp salt
- 1 tsp ground ginger
- ¼ tsp ground cinnamon
- ¼ tsp ground nutmeg
- ½ cup (115g) unsalted butter, softened
- ½ cup (100g) granulated sugar
- ½ cup (100g) packed light brown sugar
- 2 large eggs
- ½ cup (120ml) sour cream (or plain yogurt)
- 1 tsp vanilla extract
- 1-2 fresh pears, peeled, cored, and chopped (about 1 ½ cups or 200g)
- ¼ cup (30g) crystallized ginger, finely chopped (optional, for added flavor)

For the Ginger Glaze (Optional):

- ¼ cup (60ml) pear juice or water
- ¼ cup (50g) granulated sugar
- 1 tbsp finely chopped crystallized ginger

For Decoration (Optional):

- Fresh pear slices
- Additional crystallized ginger pieces
- Powdered sugar

Instructions:

1. Preheat the Oven:

- Preheat your oven to 350°F (175°C). Grease and flour a 9-inch round cake pan or line it with parchment paper.

2. Prepare the Cake Batter:

- In a medium bowl, whisk together the flour, baking powder, baking soda, salt, ground ginger, cinnamon, and nutmeg.

- In a large mixing bowl, cream the softened butter, granulated sugar, and brown sugar until light and fluffy.
- Add the eggs one at a time, beating well after each addition.
- Mix in the vanilla extract.
- Gradually add the dry ingredients to the butter mixture, alternating with the sour cream. Begin and end with the dry ingredients. Mix until just combined.
- Gently fold in the chopped pears and crystallized ginger if using.

3. Bake the Cake:

- Pour the batter into the prepared pan and smooth the top.
- Bake for 30-35 minutes, or until a toothpick inserted into the center comes out clean.
- Allow the cake to cool in the pan for 10 minutes, then turn it out onto a wire rack to cool completely.

4. Prepare the Ginger Glaze (Optional):

- In a small saucepan, combine the pear juice or water, granulated sugar, and finely chopped crystallized ginger.
- Heat over medium heat, stirring until the sugar is dissolved and the mixture is slightly thickened.
- Allow it to cool slightly before using.

5. Decorate (Optional):

- Once the cake is completely cool, you can brush it with the ginger glaze for extra flavor and shine.
- Garnish with fresh pear slices, additional crystallized ginger pieces, and a dusting of powdered sugar if desired.

6. Serve:

- Slice and enjoy your Pear and Ginger Cake!

This cake is wonderfully moist with the sweet and spicy flavors of pear and ginger, making it a perfect dessert for fall or any time you want a comforting treat. Enjoy!

Chocolate Mint Cake

Ingredients:

For the Cake:

- 1 ¾ cups (220g) all-purpose flour
- 1 ½ tsp baking powder
- ½ tsp baking soda
- ¼ tsp salt
- ½ cup (50g) unsweetened cocoa powder
- 1 cup (200g) granulated sugar
- ½ cup (100g) packed light brown sugar
- ½ cup (115g) unsalted butter, softened
- 2 large eggs
- 1 cup (240ml) buttermilk (or whole milk)
- 1 tsp vanilla extract
- 1 tsp peppermint extract (adjust to taste)

For the Chocolate Mint Frosting:

- 1 cup (225g) unsalted butter, softened
- 3 ½ cups (440g) confectioners' sugar
- ¼ cup (25g) unsweetened cocoa powder
- 2-3 tbsp milk or heavy cream (to adjust consistency)
- 1 tsp vanilla extract
- 1 tsp peppermint extract
- A pinch of salt

For Decoration (Optional):

- Crushed mint chocolate candies or peppermint candies
- Fresh mint leaves
- Chocolate shavings or curls

Instructions:

1. Preheat the Oven:

- Preheat your oven to 350°F (175°C). Grease and flour two 9-inch round cake pans or line them with parchment paper.

2. Prepare the Cake Batter:

- In a medium bowl, whisk together the flour, baking powder, baking soda, salt, and cocoa powder.

- In a large mixing bowl, cream the softened butter, granulated sugar, and brown sugar until light and fluffy.
- Add the eggs one at a time, beating well after each addition.
- Mix in the vanilla extract and peppermint extract.
- Gradually add the dry ingredients to the butter mixture, alternating with the buttermilk. Begin and end with the dry ingredients. Mix until just combined.

3. Bake the Cake:

- Divide the batter evenly between the prepared pans and smooth the tops.
- Bake for 25-30 minutes, or until a toothpick inserted into the center comes out clean.
- Allow the cakes to cool in the pans for 10 minutes, then turn them out onto a wire rack to cool completely.

4. Prepare the Chocolate Mint Frosting:

- In a large mixing bowl, beat the softened butter until creamy.
- Gradually add the confectioners' sugar and cocoa powder, mixing on low speed until combined.
- Mix in the vanilla extract, peppermint extract, and a pinch of salt.
- Add 2-3 tablespoons of milk or heavy cream to achieve a smooth, spreadable consistency. Adjust as needed.

5. Assemble the Cake:

- Once the cakes are completely cool, place one cake layer on a serving plate or cake stand.
- Spread a layer of chocolate mint frosting on top.
- Place the second cake layer on top and frost the top and sides with the remaining frosting.

6. Decorate (Optional):

- Garnish with crushed mint chocolate candies or peppermint candies, fresh mint leaves, and chocolate shavings or curls if desired.

7. Serve:

- Slice and enjoy your rich and refreshing Chocolate Mint Cake!

This cake combines the deep flavor of chocolate with the coolness of mint, creating a delightful dessert that's perfect for any occasion. Enjoy!

Mocha Almond Cake

Ingredients:

For the Cake:

- 1 ½ cups (190g) all-purpose flour
- 1 ½ tsp baking powder
- ½ tsp baking soda
- ¼ tsp salt
- ¼ cup (25g) unsweetened cocoa powder
- 1 tbsp instant coffee granules (or espresso powder)
- ½ cup (115g) unsalted butter, softened
- 1 cup (200g) granulated sugar
- ½ cup (100g) packed light brown sugar
- 2 large eggs
- ½ cup (120ml) buttermilk (or whole milk)
- ½ cup (120ml) hot brewed coffee
- 1 tsp vanilla extract
- ½ cup (60g) finely chopped almonds (toasted if desired)

For the Mocha Almond Frosting:

- 1 cup (225g) unsalted butter, softened
- 3 ½ cups (440g) confectioners' sugar
- ¼ cup (25g) unsweetened cocoa powder
- 2 tbsp instant coffee granules (or espresso powder)
- 2-3 tbsp milk or heavy cream (to adjust consistency)
- 1 tsp vanilla extract
- A pinch of salt

For Decoration (Optional):

- Toasted almond slices
- Chocolate shavings
- Whole almonds

Instructions:

1. Preheat the Oven:

- Preheat your oven to 350°F (175°C). Grease and flour two 9-inch round cake pans or line them with parchment paper.

2. Prepare the Cake Batter:

- In a medium bowl, whisk together the flour, baking powder, baking soda, salt, cocoa powder, and instant coffee granules.
- In a large mixing bowl, cream the softened butter, granulated sugar, and brown sugar until light and fluffy.
- Add the eggs one at a time, beating well after each addition.
- Mix in the vanilla extract.
- Gradually add the dry ingredients to the butter mixture, alternating with the buttermilk and hot coffee. Begin and end with the dry ingredients. Mix until just combined.
- Fold in the finely chopped almonds.

3. Bake the Cake:

- Divide the batter evenly between the prepared pans and smooth the tops.
- Bake for 25-30 minutes, or until a toothpick inserted into the center comes out clean.
- Allow the cakes to cool in the pans for 10 minutes, then turn them out onto a wire rack to cool completely.

4. Prepare the Mocha Almond Frosting:

- In a large mixing bowl, beat the softened butter until creamy.
- Gradually add the confectioners' sugar and cocoa powder, mixing on low speed until combined.
- Mix in the instant coffee granules, vanilla extract, and a pinch of salt.
- Add 2-3 tablespoons of milk or heavy cream to achieve a smooth, spreadable consistency. Adjust as needed.

5. Assemble the Cake:

- Once the cakes are completely cool, place one cake layer on a serving plate or cake stand.
- Spread a layer of mocha almond frosting on top.
- Place the second cake layer on top and frost the top and sides with the remaining frosting.

6. Decorate (Optional):

- Garnish with toasted almond slices, chocolate shavings, and whole almonds if desired.

7. Serve:

- Slice and enjoy your rich and flavorful Mocha Almond Cake!

This cake combines the robust flavors of mocha with the nutty crunch of almonds, making it a perfect treat for coffee lovers and those who enjoy a bit of sophistication in their desserts. Enjoy!

Lemon Blueberry Bundt Cake

Ingredients:

For the Cake:

- 2 ½ cups (315g) all-purpose flour
- 2 tsp baking powder
- ½ tsp baking soda
- ¼ tsp salt
- ½ cup (115g) unsalted butter, softened
- 1 cup (200g) granulated sugar
- ½ cup (100g) packed light brown sugar
- 3 large eggs
- 1 cup (240ml) buttermilk (or whole milk)
- 1 cup (240ml) fresh lemon juice (about 4 lemons)
- 2 tbsp lemon zest (from about 2 lemons)
- 1 tsp vanilla extract
- 1 ½ cups (225g) fresh or frozen blueberries (if using frozen, do not thaw)

For the Lemon Glaze:

- 1 cup (120g) confectioners' sugar
- 2-3 tbsp fresh lemon juice
- 1 tbsp lemon zest

For Decoration (Optional):

- Fresh blueberries
- Lemon zest

Instructions:

1. Preheat the Oven:

- Preheat your oven to 350°F (175°C). Grease and flour a 10-cup bundt pan or spray it with non-stick baking spray.

2. Prepare the Cake Batter:

- In a medium bowl, whisk together the flour, baking powder, baking soda, and salt.
- In a large mixing bowl, cream the softened butter, granulated sugar, and brown sugar until light and fluffy.
- Add the eggs one at a time, beating well after each addition.
- Mix in the vanilla extract, lemon juice, and lemon zest.

- Gradually add the dry ingredients to the butter mixture, alternating with the buttermilk. Begin and end with the dry ingredients. Mix until just combined.
- Gently fold in the blueberries.

3. Bake the Cake:

- Pour the batter into the prepared bundt pan and smooth the top.
- Bake for 45-55 minutes, or until a toothpick inserted into the center comes out clean.
- Allow the cake to cool in the pan for 10-15 minutes, then carefully invert it onto a wire rack to cool completely.

4. Prepare the Lemon Glaze:

- In a small bowl, whisk together the confectioners' sugar, lemon juice, and lemon zest until smooth and pourable. Adjust the consistency with more lemon juice or confectioners' sugar if needed.

5. Glaze the Cake:

- Once the cake is completely cool, drizzle the lemon glaze over the top.

6. Decorate (Optional):

- Garnish with fresh blueberries and additional lemon zest if desired.

7. Serve:

- Slice and enjoy your refreshing Lemon Blueberry Bundt Cake!

This bundt cake combines the bright flavor of lemon with sweet blueberries for a light and delicious treat that's perfect for any occasion. Enjoy!

Creamy Lime Cake

Ingredients:

For the Cake:

- 2 ½ cups (315g) all-purpose flour
- 2 tsp baking powder
- ½ tsp baking soda
- ¼ tsp salt
- ½ cup (115g) unsalted butter, softened
- 1 cup (200g) granulated sugar
- ½ cup (100g) packed light brown sugar
- 3 large eggs
- 1 cup (240ml) sour cream (or plain yogurt)
- ½ cup (120ml) fresh lime juice (about 4 limes)
- 2 tbsp lime zest (from about 2 limes)
- 1 tsp vanilla extract

For the Creamy Lime Frosting:

- 1 cup (225g) unsalted butter, softened
- 3 ½ cups (440g) confectioners' sugar
- ¼ cup (60ml) fresh lime juice
- 1-2 tbsp heavy cream or milk (to adjust consistency)
- 1 tsp vanilla extract
- 2 tbsp lime zest (for extra flavor)
- A pinch of salt

For Decoration (Optional):

- Lime zest
- Fresh lime slices
- Additional lime wedges

Instructions:

1. Preheat the Oven:

- Preheat your oven to 350°F (175°C). Grease and flour two 9-inch round cake pans or line them with parchment paper.

2. Prepare the Cake Batter:

- In a medium bowl, whisk together the flour, baking powder, baking soda, and salt.

- In a large mixing bowl, cream the softened butter, granulated sugar, and brown sugar until light and fluffy.
- Add the eggs one at a time, beating well after each addition.
- Mix in the vanilla extract, lime juice, and lime zest.
- Gradually add the dry ingredients to the butter mixture, alternating with the sour cream. Begin and end with the dry ingredients. Mix until just combined.

3. Bake the Cake:

- Divide the batter evenly between the prepared pans and smooth the tops.
- Bake for 25-30 minutes, or until a toothpick inserted into the center comes out clean.
- Allow the cakes to cool in the pans for 10 minutes, then turn them out onto a wire rack to cool completely.

4. Prepare the Creamy Lime Frosting:

- In a large mixing bowl, beat the softened butter until creamy.
- Gradually add the confectioners' sugar, mixing on low speed until combined.
- Mix in the lime juice, lime zest, and a pinch of salt.
- Add 1-2 tablespoons of heavy cream or milk to achieve a smooth, spreadable consistency. Adjust as needed.

5. Assemble the Cake:

- Once the cakes are completely cool, place one cake layer on a serving plate or cake stand.
- Spread a layer of creamy lime frosting on top.
- Place the second cake layer on top and frost the top and sides with the remaining frosting.

6. Decorate (Optional):

- Garnish with additional lime zest, fresh lime slices, or lime wedges if desired.

7. Serve:

- Slice and enjoy your tangy and creamy Lime Cake!

This Creamy Lime Cake combines the bright and refreshing flavor of lime with a rich, creamy frosting, making it a delightful dessert for any lime enthusiast. Enjoy!

Cinnamon Roll Cake

Ingredients:

For the Cake:

- 2 ¼ cups (280g) all-purpose flour
- 1 ½ tsp baking powder
- ½ tsp baking soda
- ¼ tsp salt
- ½ cup (115g) unsalted butter, softened
- 1 cup (200g) granulated sugar
- 2 large eggs
- 1 cup (240ml) buttermilk (or whole milk)
- 1 tsp vanilla extract

For the Cinnamon Swirl:

- ½ cup (115g) unsalted butter, melted
- 1 cup (200g) brown sugar
- 2 tbsp ground cinnamon

For the Vanilla Glaze:

- 1 cup (120g) confectioners' sugar
- 2-3 tbsp milk or heavy cream
- ½ tsp vanilla extract

For Decoration (Optional):

- Ground cinnamon
- Additional confectioners' sugar

Instructions:

1. Preheat the Oven:

- Preheat your oven to 350°F (175°C). Grease and flour a 9x13-inch baking pan or line it with parchment paper.

2. Prepare the Cake Batter:

- In a medium bowl, whisk together the flour, baking powder, baking soda, and salt.
- In a large mixing bowl, cream the softened butter and granulated sugar until light and fluffy.
- Add the eggs one at a time, beating well after each addition.
- Mix in the vanilla extract.

- Gradually add the dry ingredients to the butter mixture, alternating with the buttermilk. Begin and end with the dry ingredients. Mix until just combined.

3. Prepare the Cinnamon Swirl:

- In a small bowl, mix together the melted butter, brown sugar, and ground cinnamon.

4. Assemble the Cake:

- Pour half of the cake batter into the prepared pan and spread it evenly.
- Spoon the cinnamon swirl mixture over the batter in dollops, then use a knife or a toothpick to gently swirl the mixture into the batter.
- Spread the remaining cake batter over the cinnamon swirl layer.
- Use the knife or toothpick again to create a swirl pattern on the top layer.

5. Bake the Cake:

- Bake for 30-35 minutes, or until a toothpick inserted into the center comes out clean.
- Allow the cake to cool in the pan for 10 minutes, then transfer it to a wire rack to cool completely.

6. Prepare the Vanilla Glaze:

- In a small bowl, whisk together the confectioners' sugar, milk or heavy cream, and vanilla extract until smooth and pourable. Adjust the consistency with more milk or confectioners' sugar if needed.

7. Glaze the Cake:

- Once the cake is completely cool, drizzle the vanilla glaze over the top.

8. Decorate (Optional):

- Sprinkle with additional ground cinnamon or confectioners' sugar if desired.

9. Serve:

- Slice and enjoy your Cinnamon Roll Cake!

This cake combines the flavors of classic cinnamon rolls with the ease of a single-layer cake, making it a perfect breakfast treat or dessert for any occasion. Enjoy!

Espresso Cake

Ingredients:

For the Cake:

- 1 ½ cups (190g) all-purpose flour
- 1 ½ tsp baking powder
- ½ tsp baking soda
- ¼ tsp salt
- ¼ cup (25g) unsweetened cocoa powder
- 2 tbsp instant espresso granules (or finely ground espresso)
- ½ cup (115g) unsalted butter, softened
- 1 cup (200g) granulated sugar
- ½ cup (100g) packed light brown sugar
- 2 large eggs
- 1 cup (240ml) buttermilk (or whole milk)
- 1 tsp vanilla extract

For the Espresso Frosting:

- 1 cup (225g) unsalted butter, softened
- 3 ½ cups (440g) confectioners' sugar
- 2 tbsp instant espresso granules (or finely ground espresso)
- 2-3 tbsp milk or heavy cream (to adjust consistency)
- 1 tsp vanilla extract
- A pinch of salt

For Decoration (Optional):

- Chocolate shavings
- Coffee beans
- A dusting of cocoa powder

Instructions:

1. Preheat the Oven:

- Preheat your oven to 350°F (175°C). Grease and flour two 9-inch round cake pans or line them with parchment paper.

2. Prepare the Cake Batter:

- In a medium bowl, whisk together the flour, baking powder, baking soda, salt, cocoa powder, and instant espresso granules.

- In a large mixing bowl, cream the softened butter, granulated sugar, and brown sugar until light and fluffy.
- Add the eggs one at a time, beating well after each addition.
- Mix in the vanilla extract.
- Gradually add the dry ingredients to the butter mixture, alternating with the buttermilk. Begin and end with the dry ingredients. Mix until just combined.

3. Bake the Cake:

- Divide the batter evenly between the prepared pans and smooth the tops.
- Bake for 25-30 minutes, or until a toothpick inserted into the center comes out clean.
- Allow the cakes to cool in the pans for 10 minutes, then turn them out onto a wire rack to cool completely.

4. Prepare the Espresso Frosting:

- In a large mixing bowl, beat the softened butter until creamy.
- Gradually add the confectioners' sugar and instant espresso granules, mixing on low speed until fully incorporated.
- Mix in the vanilla extract and a pinch of salt.
- Add 2-3 tablespoons of milk or heavy cream to achieve a smooth, spreadable consistency. Adjust as needed.

5. Assemble the Cake:

- Once the cakes are completely cool, place one cake layer on a serving plate or cake stand.
- Spread a layer of espresso frosting on top.
- Place the second cake layer on top and frost the top and sides with the remaining frosting.

6. Decorate (Optional):

- Garnish with chocolate shavings, coffee beans, or a dusting of cocoa powder if desired.

7. Serve:

- Slice and enjoy your rich and flavorful Espresso Cake!

This cake has a deep coffee flavor that's complemented by the creamy espresso frosting, making it a perfect dessert for coffee enthusiasts. Enjoy!

Chocolate Cherry Cake

Ingredients:

For the Cake:

- 1 ½ cups (190g) all-purpose flour
- 1 ½ tsp baking powder
- ½ tsp baking soda
- ¼ tsp salt
- ½ cup (50g) unsweetened cocoa powder
- 1 cup (200g) granulated sugar
- ½ cup (100g) packed light brown sugar
- ½ cup (115g) unsalted butter, softened
- 2 large eggs
- 1 cup (240ml) buttermilk (or whole milk)
- 1 tsp vanilla extract
- 1 cup (150g) fresh or frozen pitted cherries, chopped (if using frozen, do not thaw)

For the Cherry Filling:

- 1 cup (150g) fresh or frozen pitted cherries, chopped
- ¼ cup (50g) granulated sugar
- 1 tbsp cornstarch
- 1 tbsp lemon juice

For the Chocolate Ganache:

- 1 cup (240ml) heavy cream
- 8 oz (225g) semisweet chocolate, chopped
- 1 tbsp unsalted butter

For Decoration (Optional):

- Fresh cherries
- Chocolate shavings or curls

Instructions:

1. Prepare the Cherry Filling:

- In a small saucepan, combine the chopped cherries, granulated sugar, cornstarch, and lemon juice.
- Cook over medium heat, stirring frequently, until the mixture thickens and the cherries are softened, about 5-7 minutes.
- Let it cool to room temperature.

2. Preheat the Oven:

- Preheat your oven to 350°F (175°C). Grease and flour two 9-inch round cake pans or line them with parchment paper.

3. Prepare the Cake Batter:

- In a medium bowl, whisk together the flour, baking powder, baking soda, salt, and cocoa powder.
- In a large mixing bowl, cream the softened butter, granulated sugar, and brown sugar until light and fluffy.
- Add the eggs one at a time, beating well after each addition.
- Mix in the vanilla extract.
- Gradually add the dry ingredients to the butter mixture, alternating with the buttermilk. Begin and end with the dry ingredients. Mix until just combined.
- Gently fold in the chopped cherries.

4. Bake the Cake:

- Divide the batter evenly between the prepared pans and smooth the tops.
- Bake for 25-30 minutes, or until a toothpick inserted into the center comes out clean.
- Allow the cakes to cool in the pans for 10 minutes, then turn them out onto a wire rack to cool completely.

5. Prepare the Chocolate Ganache:

- Heat the heavy cream in a small saucepan over medium heat until it just begins to simmer.
- Remove from heat and add the chopped chocolate, stirring until smooth.
- Stir in the butter until melted and smooth. Let it cool slightly before using.

6. Assemble the Cake:

- Once the cakes are completely cool, place one cake layer on a serving plate or cake stand.
- Spread the cherry filling evenly over the cake layer.
- Place the second cake layer on top and frost the top and sides with the chocolate ganache.

7. Decorate (Optional):

- Garnish with fresh cherries and chocolate shavings or curls if desired.

8. Serve:

- Slice and enjoy your indulgent Chocolate Cherry Cake!

This cake combines the richness of chocolate with the bright, fruity flavor of cherries, creating a delicious and elegant dessert. Enjoy!

Pineapple Upside-Down Cake

Ingredients:

For the Topping:

- ¼ cup (60g) unsalted butter
- ½ cup (100g) packed light brown sugar
- 1 can (20 oz or 565g) sliced pineapple, drained (reserve the juice)
- 10-12 maraschino cherries (optional)

For the Cake:

- 1 ¼ cups (155g) all-purpose flour
- 1 ½ tsp baking powder
- ¼ tsp salt
- ¼ cup (50g) granulated sugar
- ¼ cup (50g) packed light brown sugar
- ½ cup (115g) unsalted butter, softened
- 2 large eggs
- ½ cup (120ml) pineapple juice (from the canned pineapple)
- 1 tsp vanilla extract

Instructions:

1. Preheat the Oven:

- Preheat your oven to 350°F (175°C). Grease and flour a 9-inch round cake pan or line it with parchment paper.

2. Prepare the Topping:

- In a medium saucepan, melt the butter over medium heat.
- Stir in the brown sugar until dissolved and the mixture is bubbly.
- Pour the caramel mixture into the bottom of the prepared cake pan, spreading it evenly.
- Arrange the pineapple slices over the caramel, placing a cherry in the center of each pineapple slice if using.

3. Prepare the Cake Batter:

- In a medium bowl, whisk together the flour, baking powder, and salt.
- In a large mixing bowl, cream the softened butter, granulated sugar, and brown sugar until light and fluffy.
- Add the eggs one at a time, beating well after each addition.
- Mix in the vanilla extract.

- Gradually add the dry ingredients to the butter mixture, alternating with the pineapple juice. Begin and end with the dry ingredients. Mix until just combined.

4. Bake the Cake:

- Pour the batter evenly over the pineapple topping in the cake pan.
- Smooth the top and bake for 35-40 minutes, or until a toothpick inserted into the center comes out clean.
- Allow the cake to cool in the pan for 10 minutes, then carefully invert it onto a serving plate or cake stand.

5. Serve:

- Slice and enjoy your Pineapple Upside-Down Cake warm or at room temperature!

This cake is a delightful blend of caramelized pineapple and sweet cake, perfect for a nostalgic dessert or special occasion. Enjoy!

Champagne Cake

Ingredients:

For the Cake:

- 1 ¾ cups (220g) all-purpose flour
- 1 ½ tsp baking powder
- ¼ tsp salt
- ½ cup (115g) unsalted butter, softened
- 1 cup (200g) granulated sugar
- 2 large eggs
- 1 cup (240ml) champagne (chilled, any variety)
- 1 tsp vanilla extract

For the Champagne Frosting:

- 1 cup (225g) unsalted butter, softened
- 3 ½ cups (440g) confectioners' sugar
- ¼ cup (60ml) champagne (chilled)
- 1 tsp vanilla extract
- A pinch of salt

For Decoration (Optional):

- Edible gold leaf
- Fresh berries

Instructions:

1. Preheat the Oven:

- Preheat your oven to 350°F (175°C). Grease and flour two 9-inch round cake pans or line them with parchment paper.

2. Prepare the Cake Batter:

- In a medium bowl, whisk together the flour, baking powder, and salt.
- In a large mixing bowl, cream the softened butter and granulated sugar until light and fluffy.
- Add the eggs one at a time, beating well after each addition.
- Mix in the vanilla extract.
- Gradually add the dry ingredients to the butter mixture, alternating with the champagne. Begin and end with the dry ingredients. Mix until just combined.

3. Bake the Cake:

- Divide the batter evenly between the prepared pans and smooth the tops.
- Bake for 25-30 minutes, or until a toothpick inserted into the center comes out clean.
- Allow the cakes to cool in the pans for 10 minutes, then turn them out onto a wire rack to cool completely.

4. Prepare the Champagne Frosting:

- In a large mixing bowl, beat the softened butter until creamy.
- Gradually add the confectioners' sugar, mixing on low speed until incorporated.
- Mix in the champagne, vanilla extract, and a pinch of salt. Beat until smooth and fluffy.

5. Assemble the Cake:

- Once the cakes are completely cool, place one cake layer on a serving plate or cake stand.
- Spread a layer of champagne frosting on top.
- Place the second cake layer on top and frost the top and sides with the remaining frosting.

6. Decorate (Optional):

- Garnish with edible gold leaf and fresh berries if desired.

7. Serve:

- Slice and enjoy your sophisticated Champagne Cake!

This cake offers a delicate champagne flavor with a light, airy texture, making it a delightful choice for special occasions or celebrations. Enjoy!

Sweet Potato Cake

Ingredients:

For the Cake:

- 1 ½ cups (190g) all-purpose flour
- 1 tsp baking powder
- ½ tsp baking soda
- ½ tsp salt
- 1 tsp ground cinnamon
- ½ tsp ground nutmeg
- ¼ tsp ground cloves
- ½ cup (115g) unsalted butter, softened
- 1 cup (200g) granulated sugar
- ½ cup (100g) packed light brown sugar
- 2 large eggs
- 1 cup (240ml) mashed sweet potato (about 1 medium sweet potato, cooked and pureed)
- ½ cup (120ml) buttermilk (or whole milk)
- 1 tsp vanilla extract

For the Cream Cheese Frosting:

- 8 oz (225g) cream cheese, softened
- ¼ cup (60g) unsalted butter, softened
- 3 ½ cups (440g) confectioners' sugar
- 1 tsp vanilla extract
- A pinch of salt

For Decoration (Optional):

- Chopped pecans
- Ground cinnamon

Instructions:

1. Preheat the Oven:

- Preheat your oven to 350°F (175°C). Grease and flour two 9-inch round cake pans or line them with parchment paper.

2. Prepare the Cake Batter:

- In a medium bowl, whisk together the flour, baking powder, baking soda, salt, cinnamon, nutmeg, and cloves.

- In a large mixing bowl, cream the softened butter, granulated sugar, and brown sugar until light and fluffy.
- Add the eggs one at a time, beating well after each addition.
- Mix in the mashed sweet potato, buttermilk, and vanilla extract.
- Gradually add the dry ingredients to the wet mixture, mixing until just combined.

3. Bake the Cake:

- Divide the batter evenly between the prepared pans and smooth the tops.
- Bake for 25-30 minutes, or until a toothpick inserted into the center comes out clean.
- Allow the cakes to cool in the pans for 10 minutes, then turn them out onto a wire rack to cool completely.

4. Prepare the Cream Cheese Frosting:

- In a large mixing bowl, beat the softened cream cheese and butter until smooth and creamy.
- Gradually add the confectioners' sugar, mixing on low speed until combined.
- Mix in the vanilla extract and a pinch of salt until smooth.

5. Assemble the Cake:

- Once the cakes are completely cool, place one layer on a serving plate or cake stand.
- Spread a layer of cream cheese frosting on top.
- Place the second cake layer on top and frost the top and sides with the remaining frosting.

6. Decorate (Optional):

- Garnish with chopped pecans and a dusting of ground cinnamon if desired.

7. Serve:

- Slice and enjoy your delicious Sweet Potato Cake!

This cake combines the rich flavor of sweet potatoes with warm spices and a creamy frosting, making it a comforting and delightful dessert. Enjoy!

Nutella Swirl Cake

Ingredients:

For the Cake:

- 1 ¾ cups (220g) all-purpose flour
- 1 ½ tsp baking powder
- ½ tsp baking soda
- ¼ tsp salt
- ½ cup (115g) unsalted butter, softened
- 1 cup (200g) granulated sugar
- 2 large eggs
- 1 cup (240ml) buttermilk (or whole milk)
- 1 tsp vanilla extract
- ½ cup (140g) Nutella (or any chocolate-hazelnut spread)

For the Nutella Swirl:

- ¼ cup (70g) Nutella (or chocolate-hazelnut spread)

For Decoration (Optional):

- Powdered sugar
- Chopped hazelnuts

Instructions:

1. Preheat the Oven:

- Preheat your oven to 350°F (175°C). Grease and flour a 9-inch round cake pan or line it with parchment paper.

2. Prepare the Cake Batter:

- In a medium bowl, whisk together the flour, baking powder, baking soda, and salt.
- In a large mixing bowl, cream the softened butter and granulated sugar until light and fluffy.
- Add the eggs one at a time, beating well after each addition.
- Mix in the vanilla extract.
- Gradually add the dry ingredients to the butter mixture, alternating with the buttermilk. Begin and end with the dry ingredients. Mix until just combined.

3. Prepare the Nutella Swirl:

- Gently heat the Nutella in the microwave for about 20 seconds to make it easier to swirl.

4. Assemble the Cake:

- Pour half of the cake batter into the prepared pan and smooth the top.
- Spoon half of the Nutella over the batter in dollops.
- Add the remaining batter on top, then spoon the remaining Nutella over the top.
- Use a knife or toothpick to gently swirl the Nutella into the batter, creating a marble effect.

5. Bake the Cake:

- Bake for 30-35 minutes, or until a toothpick inserted into the center comes out clean.
- Allow the cake to cool in the pan for 10 minutes, then turn it out onto a wire rack to cool completely.

6. Decorate (Optional):

- Dust with powdered sugar and sprinkle with chopped hazelnuts if desired.

7. Serve:

- Slice and enjoy your Nutella Swirl Cake!

This cake combines the rich flavors of Nutella with a moist, tender crumb, making it a delightful treat for any chocolate lover. Enjoy!

Strawberry Basil Cake

Ingredients:

For the Cake:

- 1 ¾ cups (220g) all-purpose flour
- 1 ½ tsp baking powder
- ¼ tsp baking soda
- ¼ tsp salt
- ½ cup (115g) unsalted butter, softened
- 1 cup (200g) granulated sugar
- 2 large eggs
- 1 cup (240ml) buttermilk (or whole milk)
- 1 tsp vanilla extract
- ½ cup (125g) finely chopped fresh strawberries
- ¼ cup (15g) finely chopped fresh basil leaves

For the Strawberry Basil Frosting:

- 1 cup (225g) unsalted butter, softened
- 3 ½ cups (440g) confectioners' sugar
- ¼ cup (60ml) milk or heavy cream
- ½ cup (125g) pureed fresh strawberries
- 1 tbsp finely chopped fresh basil leaves
- 1 tsp vanilla extract
- A pinch of salt

For Decoration (Optional):

- Fresh strawberries
- Basil leaves

Instructions:

1. Preheat the Oven:

- Preheat your oven to 350°F (175°C). Grease and flour two 9-inch round cake pans or line them with parchment paper.

2. Prepare the Cake Batter:

- In a medium bowl, whisk together the flour, baking powder, baking soda, and salt.
- In a large mixing bowl, cream the softened butter and granulated sugar until light and fluffy.
- Add the eggs one at a time, beating well after each addition.

- Mix in the vanilla extract.
- Gradually add the dry ingredients to the butter mixture, alternating with the buttermilk. Begin and end with the dry ingredients. Mix until just combined.
- Gently fold in the chopped strawberries and basil.

3. Bake the Cake:

- Divide the batter evenly between the prepared pans and smooth the tops.
- Bake for 25-30 minutes, or until a toothpick inserted into the center comes out clean.
- Allow the cakes to cool in the pans for 10 minutes, then turn them out onto a wire rack to cool completely.

4. Prepare the Strawberry Basil Frosting:

- In a large mixing bowl, beat the softened butter until creamy.
- Gradually add the confectioners' sugar, mixing on low speed until combined.
- Mix in the milk or heavy cream, strawberry puree, chopped basil, and vanilla extract. Beat until smooth and fluffy. Adjust the consistency with more milk or sugar if needed.

5. Assemble the Cake:

- Once the cakes are completely cool, place one layer on a serving plate or cake stand.
- Spread a layer of strawberry basil frosting on top.
- Place the second cake layer on top and frost the top and sides with the remaining frosting.

6. Decorate (Optional):

- Garnish with fresh strawberries and basil leaves if desired.

7. Serve:

- Slice and enjoy your Strawberry Basil Cake!

This cake combines the fresh flavors of strawberries and basil, creating a delightful and unique dessert experience. Enjoy!

Raspberry Lemonade Cake

Ingredients:

For the Cake:

- 1 ¾ cups (220g) all-purpose flour
- 1 ½ tsp baking powder
- ¼ tsp baking soda
- ¼ tsp salt
- ½ cup (115g) unsalted butter, softened
- 1 cup (200g) granulated sugar
- 2 large eggs
- ½ cup (120ml) freshly squeezed lemon juice (about 2 lemons)
- ½ cup (120ml) milk (whole or buttermilk)
- 1 tsp vanilla extract
- ½ cup (125g) fresh raspberries (or frozen, thawed)

For the Raspberry Lemonade Frosting:

- 1 cup (225g) unsalted butter, softened
- 3 ½ cups (440g) confectioners' sugar
- ¼ cup (60ml) freshly squeezed lemon juice
- ¼ cup (60ml) raspberry puree (blend fresh or frozen raspberries and strain)
- 1 tsp vanilla extract
- A pinch of salt

For Decoration (Optional):

- Fresh raspberries
- Lemon zest
- Mint leaves

Instructions:

1. Preheat the Oven:

- Preheat your oven to 350°F (175°C). Grease and flour two 9-inch round cake pans or line them with parchment paper.

2. Prepare the Cake Batter:

- In a medium bowl, whisk together the flour, baking powder, baking soda, and salt.
- In a large mixing bowl, cream the softened butter and granulated sugar until light and fluffy.
- Add the eggs one at a time, beating well after each addition.

- Mix in the vanilla extract.
- Gradually add the dry ingredients to the butter mixture, alternating with the lemon juice and milk. Begin and end with the dry ingredients. Mix until just combined.
- Gently fold in the raspberries.

3. Bake the Cake:

- Divide the batter evenly between the prepared pans and smooth the tops.
- Bake for 25-30 minutes, or until a toothpick inserted into the center comes out clean.
- Allow the cakes to cool in the pans for 10 minutes, then turn them out onto a wire rack to cool completely.

4. Prepare the Raspberry Lemonade Frosting:

- In a large mixing bowl, beat the softened butter until creamy.
- Gradually add the confectioners' sugar, mixing on low speed until fully incorporated.
- Mix in the lemon juice, raspberry puree, vanilla extract, and a pinch of salt. Beat until smooth and fluffy. Adjust the consistency with more sugar or lemon juice if needed.

5. Assemble the Cake:

- Once the cakes are completely cool, place one layer on a serving plate or cake stand.
- Spread a layer of raspberry lemonade frosting on top.
- Place the second cake layer on top and frost the top and sides with the remaining frosting.

6. Decorate (Optional):

- Garnish with fresh raspberries, lemon zest, and mint leaves if desired.

7. Serve:

- Slice and enjoy your refreshing Raspberry Lemonade Cake!

This cake features a delightful balance of tart lemon and sweet raspberry flavors, making it a perfect treat for warm weather or special celebrations. Enjoy!

Cardamom Cake

Ingredients:

For the Cake:

- 1 ½ cups (190g) all-purpose flour
- 1 ½ tsp baking powder
- ½ tsp baking soda
- ¼ tsp salt
- 1 ½ tsp ground cardamom
- ½ cup (115g) unsalted butter, softened
- 1 cup (200g) granulated sugar
- 2 large eggs
- 1 cup (240ml) buttermilk (or whole milk)
- 1 tsp vanilla extract

For the Cardamom Glaze:

- 1 cup (120g) confectioners' sugar
- 2 tbsp milk
- ½ tsp ground cardamom
- ½ tsp vanilla extract

For Decoration (Optional):

- Whole cardamom pods
- Fresh fruit (such as berries or citrus slices)

Instructions:

1. Preheat the Oven:

- Preheat your oven to 350°F (175°C). Grease and flour a 9-inch round cake pan or line it with parchment paper.

2. Prepare the Cake Batter:

- In a medium bowl, whisk together the flour, baking powder, baking soda, salt, and ground cardamom.
- In a large mixing bowl, cream the softened butter and granulated sugar until light and fluffy.
- Add the eggs one at a time, beating well after each addition.
- Mix in the vanilla extract.
- Gradually add the dry ingredients to the butter mixture, alternating with the buttermilk. Begin and end with the dry ingredients. Mix until just combined.

3. Bake the Cake:

- Pour the batter into the prepared pan and smooth the top.
- Bake for 25-30 minutes, or until a toothpick inserted into the center comes out clean.
- Allow the cake to cool in the pan for 10 minutes, then turn it out onto a wire rack to cool completely.

4. Prepare the Cardamom Glaze:

- In a small bowl, whisk together the confectioners' sugar, milk, ground cardamom, and vanilla extract until smooth. Adjust the consistency with more milk if necessary.

5. Glaze the Cake:

- Once the cake is completely cool, drizzle the cardamom glaze over the top, allowing it to drip down the sides.

6. Decorate (Optional):

- Garnish with whole cardamom pods and fresh fruit if desired.

7. Serve:

- Slice and enjoy your fragrant Cardamom Cake!

This cake is subtly spiced with cardamom, providing a delightful and aromatic twist on a classic cake. It pairs beautifully with a cup of tea or coffee. Enjoy!

Dulce de Leche Cake

Ingredients:

For the Cake:

- 1 ¾ cups (220g) all-purpose flour
- 1 ½ tsp baking powder
- ¼ tsp baking soda
- ¼ tsp salt
- ½ cup (115g) unsalted butter, softened
- 1 cup (200g) granulated sugar
- 2 large eggs
- 1 cup (240ml) sour cream (or buttermilk)
- ½ cup (120ml) dulce de leche
- 1 tsp vanilla extract

For the Dulce de Leche Frosting:

- 1 cup (225g) unsalted butter, softened
- 2 cups (250g) confectioners' sugar
- ½ cup (120ml) dulce de leche
- 1-2 tbsp milk (if needed for consistency)
- 1 tsp vanilla extract
- A pinch of salt

For Decoration (Optional):

- Extra dulce de leche for drizzling
- Chopped nuts (such as pecans or walnuts)

Instructions:

1. Preheat the Oven:

- Preheat your oven to 350°F (175°C). Grease and flour two 9-inch round cake pans or line them with parchment paper.

2. Prepare the Cake Batter:

- In a medium bowl, whisk together the flour, baking powder, baking soda, and salt.
- In a large mixing bowl, cream the softened butter and granulated sugar until light and fluffy.
- Add the eggs one at a time, beating well after each addition.
- Mix in the vanilla extract and dulce de leche.

- Gradually add the dry ingredients to the butter mixture, alternating with the sour cream. Begin and end with the dry ingredients. Mix until just combined.

3. Bake the Cake:

- Divide the batter evenly between the prepared pans and smooth the tops.
- Bake for 25-30 minutes, or until a toothpick inserted into the center comes out clean.
- Allow the cakes to cool in the pans for 10 minutes, then turn them out onto a wire rack to cool completely.

4. Prepare the Dulce de Leche Frosting:

- In a large mixing bowl, beat the softened butter until creamy.
- Gradually add the confectioners' sugar, mixing on low speed until combined.
- Mix in the dulce de leche, vanilla extract, and a pinch of salt. Beat until smooth and fluffy. Adjust the consistency with milk if needed.

5. Assemble the Cake:

- Once the cakes are completely cool, place one layer on a serving plate or cake stand.
- Spread a layer of dulce de leche frosting on top.
- Place the second cake layer on top and frost the top and sides with the remaining frosting.

6. Decorate (Optional):

- Drizzle extra dulce de leche over the top and sprinkle with chopped nuts if desired.

7. Serve:

- Slice and enjoy your delicious Dulce de Leche Cake!

This cake offers a rich, caramel flavor with a creamy frosting that's sure to impress. Enjoy every sweet bite!

www.ingramcontent.com/pod-product-compliance
Lightning Source LLC
LaVergne TN
LVHW081556060526
838201LV00054B/1908